PEACE AND VALUE EDUCATION

Contents

PEACE
AND
VALUE EDUCATION

By

M. Brindhamani
Vice Principal
Vidhya Sagar College of
Education for Women
Chengalpattu
Tamil Nadu
(INDIA)

&

T. Manichander
Research Scholar
Faculty of Education
Osmania University
Hyderabad
Andhra Pradesh
(INDIA)

DPH

DISCOVERY PUBLISHING HOUSE PVT. LTD.
NEW DELHI-110 002

Published by:

Tilak Wasan

DISCOVERY PUBLISHING HOUSE PVT. LTD.
4383/4B, Ansari Road, Darya Ganj
New Delhi - 110 002 (India)
Phone : +91-11-23279245, 43596064-65
Fax : +91-11-23253475
E-mail : discoverypublishinghouse@gmail.com
sales@discoverypublishinggroup.com

web : www.discoverypublishinggroup.com

First Edition: **2015**

ISBN: 978-93-5056-713-5

Peace and Value Education

Printed at:
Infinity Imaging Systems
Delhi

Foreword

The need for peace and value education has over the last few decades, grown enormously all over the world. Peace and value education is a worldwide movement today. Each and every individual wants to get peace. Peace is the first and supreme human value. Peace is a prerequisite of true development at all levels and in all walks of life. The ultimate peace can be achieved only by value education. This book is a simple and easy understanding of the concept of peace and value education. It touches upon almost each and every aspect of peace and value education specially focusing on researches in the field of peace education or value education. A number of examples are given, to make the basic concept clear and of use to students, teachers, and to scholars.

The book starts with a general introduction of peace and its relevance to the global scenario than it classify peace in to positive and negative peace. It also offers Indian thought to minimize the negative peace and presents the role of UNESO in the enrichment of peace in unit first.

The second Chapter deals with different types of values in organizational climate and the role of community, school and family in the development of values. In the third Chapter the book provides beautifully the definitions of peace, its teaching methods, scope, and theory of peace education. The most beautiful and unique aspect of this book is that it promotes researches in the field of peace education which is commendable.

The forth Chapter is the detail treatment of value education, this unit provides in depth coverage of value education. It beautifully discusses fundamental rights, and the role of a teaching in providing value education. It also lays emphasis on organizing researches in the field of value education, which is of great use for students, teachers and scholars.

Chapter fifth is the based upon the importance of peace and value education. Taking these factors into account, it is hoped, that this book will prove useful for all thinker, scholars and peace lovers. It is intended to serve needs of the present scenario. My best wishes to the writers and prayers to almighty for the book to be a great success.

Dr. Harendra Singh
Professor & Principal
R.N. (P.G.) Institute of
Modern Management Education &
Research Centre, C.C.S. University,
Meerut, Uttar Pradesh
(INDIA)

Preface

Peace and Value Education are now well recognised within international legal instruments and within critical educational literature as an important aspect of education. Despite this, little attention has been given in the critical literature to the philosophical foundations for peace education and the rationale for peace education thus remains substantially an assumed one. This book explores some possible ethico-philosophical foundations for peace education and value education. This book explores conceptual frameworks and methodological approaches applicable in the research of globalisation, democracy, multiculturalism and values education. We have examine central discourses surrounding peace and value education. We further illustrate how the relationship between globalisation, values education and education policy affects current models and trends in education globally. Demonstrates ideological imperatives of globalisation and its impact on peace and values education. We employ a number of diverse paradigms in peace and value education research, ranging from critical theory to globalisation. By focusing on ideology, globalisation, need and reality we attempt to examine critically both the reasons for, and the outcomes of education reforms in the domain of teaching values education, Peace Education. In doing so, we provide a more informed critique of driven models of accountability, quality and effectiveness.

Authors

1

PEACE

Peace

> *"Peace is a journey of a thousand miles and it must be taken one step at a time".*
>
> **– Lyndon B. Johnson**

Peace has always been among humanity's highest values – for some, supreme. Consider: 'Peace at any price' (Alphonse de Lamartine, Meditations Poetiques (1820). "The most disadvantageous peace is better than the most just war" (Desiderius Erasmus, Adagio). 'Peace is more important than all justice' (Martin Luther, 1530). "I prefer the most unjust peace to the justest war that was ever waged" (Cicero, Letters to Atticus). 'There never was a good war or a bad peace' (Benjamin Franklin, Letter to Josiah Quincy (September 11, 1773).

Yet, we agree little on what is peace. Perhaps the most popular (Western) view is as an absence of dissension, violence, or war, a meaning found in the New Testament and possibly an original meaning of the Greek word for peace, Irene. Pacifists have adopted this interpretation, for to them all violence is bad. This meaning is widely accepted among irenologists and students of international relations. Peace, however, are also seen as concord, or harmony and tranquility. It is viewed as peace of mind or serenity, especially in the East. It is defined as a state of law or civil government, a state of justice or goodness, a balance or equilibrium of Powers.

Such meanings of peace function at different levels. Peace may be opposed to or an opposite of antagonistic conflict, violence, or war. It may refer to an internal state (of mind or of nations) or to external relations. Or it may be narrow in conception, referring to specific relations in a particular situation (like a peace treaty), or overarching, covering a whole society (as in a world peace). Peace may be a dichotomy (it exists or it does not) or continuous, passive or active, empirical or abstract, descriptive or normative, or positive or negative.

The problem is, of course, that peace derives its meaning and qualities within a theory or framework. Christian, Hindu, or Buddhist will see peace differently, as will pacifist or internationalist. Socialist, fascist, and libertarian have different perspectives, as do power or idealistic theorists of international relations. In this diversity of meanings, peace is no different from such concepts as: justice, freedom, equality, power, conflict, class, and, indeed, any other concept. Peace is thereby locked into a descriptive or explanatory view of our reality and each other. Peace embodies a number of psychological principles, such as subjectivity, intentionality, free will, and individualism.

Within 'peace' is defined not just as the absence of war (negative peace), but also the presence of the conditions for a just and sustainable peace, including access to food and clean drinking water, education for women and children, security from physical harm, and other inviolable human rights (positive peace). This idea is rooted in the under standing that a 'just peace' is the only sustainable kind of peace; an approach that seeks merely to 'stop the guns' while ignoring the denial of human rights and unjust social and political conditions will not work in the long-run.

Sources of Peace

In antiquity two of the major systems of peace policy, the balance of power and the power monopoly systems found clear expressions in Hellas and in Rome, in the complex relations between the various Greek states on the one hand and in the pax romana system on the other. This type of peace was enforced from above and gradually took the form of the pax ecclesia system with the Pope as an arbiter, based on the special type of allegiance towards him and the hierarchy that the belief in Catholicism would engender. This led to a very mono centric Christian world, and with the Protestant reformation, or rather revolution; it is natural that balance of power thinking came to the foreground as a concept that would preserve autonomy and peace. It can be discussed whether the reformation came about as a doctrinal rationalization of drives for autonomy and/or other socio-economic forces, or whether these efforts to redistribute power and resources as an outcome of the new ideas.

Both perspectives are probably correct and useful but there were also other forces contributing to the rise of balance of power philosophies at that period, such as the Italian city state system (for instance the relation between the League of Venice and Charles VIII). In the period from the Renaissance to the French revolution balance of power thinking became crystallized and obtained a form surprisingly similar to what is found in modern strategic analysis. It became systematic policy with the Peace of Westphalia, and has played a dominant role ever since. But there are also other trends in the thinking that are more clearly peace-directed.

In the beginning of the 14th century proposals for international organizations or associations of states for the maintenance of peace emerged for the first time. During the next four centuries we can roughly distinguish between two approaches to the problem which fought for prevalence. The first would be a continuation of the power monopoly approach that is the idea that Europe should be organized as a single political system maintained by a single political authority, consisting of one or more states, with more or less a monopoly of power.

The other approach could be designated the federal approach, that is the idea that Europe should be organized as an international organization of separate states, on an equal basis. Almost every thinker concerned with this problem in this period has elements of both the federal and the power monopoly idea in his writings. Almost everybody makes proposals for some kind of union of nations or common council with some central authority, but the power monopoly idea is predominant in most of them Dubois (1305-1307) in De Recuperatione wanted a federation of Christian, sovereign states, with a council of nations to decide, a system of judges, the Pope as a final arbiter, and boycott against aggressive nations. He even suggested international schools to train personnel, an idea not yet fully realised. He rejected world government under a single authority however, and it looks as if his Common Council should be somehow under the control of the king of France.

Dante (1310) in Dc Monarchia wanted Europe to be "a unique princedom extending over all persons in time". To him it was of major importance that Heaven and Earth should be somehow being isomorphic: since there was one Mover, one Law in Heaven, then this should also be the case on Earth. But this should only apply to the international system, there should be local rule otherwise Pax Romana was his inspiration, and he took the fact that Christ was born under Augustus as a sign of divine acceptance of the pax romana system. Campanella (1600) advocated the world dominion of Spain, later of France. Leibnizurged every prince to accept the Holy Roman Emperor as their head. And ducde Sully's Grand Design was in one particular connection essentially a plan for the establishment of Wrench hegemony in Europe.

On the other side Emeric Cruce' (1623) was concerned exclusively with the federal idea and criticized the search for political control of all Europe. During this same period it is also possible to distinguish between the thinkers as to what was their main aim. All the thinkers before Cruce' were primarily concerned – not with peace, but with European unity. They advocated some sort of association between Christian states to keep order in Europe and to wage war against Turkey or Russia. Peace was at best a by-product.

One example is the very interesting system suggested under the name of George Podebrad of Bohemia (1450): he wanted an international parliament where each nation had one vote, with both assembly and tribunal, and rotating meeting-places and staff to avoid domination by one power. One of his concerns was to limit the powers of the Pope, another to unite against the Turks. Cruce' was the first to search for peace as the main goal, and characteristically he advocated the membership of all the nations of the known world: Turkey, Persia, China; Ethiopia, the East and the West Indies – in addition to the European countries. With the writings of William Penn, John Bellarsand H. De Saint-Pierreat the end of the 17th and in the beginning of the 18th century the federal approach became predominant. They all proposed to establish some sort of international organization with a rather extensive authority. At the same time their proposals were the first – apart from Cruce's – whose primary object was the maintenance of peace. Throughout the first half of the 18th century they got several followers and the federal approach became almost universally accepted.

But in the second half of that century their proposals were equally universally rejected as unattainable, unwanted or unnecessary. The philosophers from Frederick the Great to Voltaire dismissed the plan of Saint-Pierre as impracticable. And Rousseau, who examined this plan very closely, rejected it in the end as 'ar absurd dream'. Kant demanded the law of nations to be based upon a federalism of free states, but he did not accept any central authority of the 'federation'.

Bentham, who was to influence the Anglo-Saxon thoughts on the subject to a considerable extent, felt that the causes of war between states had already almost disappeared and that the rest of what might be done would be attained by appeal to reason, to law and public opinion. He wanted to reduce the power of governments within the states, not act to increase the power of governments on the international Level.

The thinking about peace after 1919 shows many different trends, which is natural, since so many ideas had by that time been tried and been shown to be at least not unconditionally valid. For this reason we shall prefer a systematic rather than a chronological presentation, since we are more concerned with the structure of such thinking than with its origin, genealogy and patterns of influence, and turn first to the concept of 'peace' itself.

Relevancy of Peace Relating to the Present Global Scenario

When peace comes to our minds we think about a world without problems, we think about a beautiful world without weapons and conflicts, where peace flourishes in all its meanings to different people, but that world may be unreachable if we do not maintain peace in our lives. Since ancient times it was so difficult to have peace because power was unstable and people were struggling for resources. This continued into the 19th century and during the 20th century. It was still so difficult for peace to flourish because of civil wars and the *First* and *Second* World War. People can break out in war and forget about peace for simple things like: money, religion, respect, or for natural resources. One cannot imagine a world without wars, and how beautiful it could be. But, people will never have peace if they do not work together to keep peace in the world, people should work together, and make peace more than just a lovely term, but something people apply in their lives. But, today the world is finding some peace in many ways. Peace is not an outdated concept for anyone and it will never be outdated. Peace has helped people survive the Holocaust, it has helped people escape slavery; it has helped people end wars and has helped many live their lives. The best way to create peace and keep it going is through education and studying other peoples' ways of life; that way people understand others' behavior and empathise with them.

Throughout history, people have fought wars because of disagreements over money, religion or natural resources. Aristotle once said: "It is not enough to win a war; it is more important to organize the peace". He describes how people fight wars and expect that, in the end, they will gain peace. This is impossible; rather, people should not fight wars to find peace, they should organize peace without wars. It is important to build peace in the world, because our population is growing and we are challenged with more problems because of many different factors. In the past, if people had learned more about other cultures and studied their history, there would have been fewer wars because they would be smarter and work together to divide resources and materials rather than fight over them. Maybe, with a good education, millions of Jewish people would not have been killed by the Nazis because they would have learned about their lives and understood what it was like to be Jewish. Today, the world is continuing to grow and this presents more challenges, because the population is increasing and more and more people need education. Education is one of the best methods to find peace because it makes.

Learning to make a living is not the sole reason for getting education; there is another, equally important byproduct: learning to make a life, a life that is beneficial, useful and peaceful. After all, humans are social animals; their success in life is largely a matter of successful social relations. Quite evidently, student age is the crucially important period which enriches one's personal life, nurtures social adjustments, fosters friendship and understanding and affects one's whole life pattern. Seen from this perspective, one could very well understand the critical necessity of teaching students, youth and young leaders the art of living together, in mutual respect, justice, love and peace.

Aristotle presents a praxio logical perspective, which connects just acts with peaceful ones. This connection is essential, for justice is a necessary condition for peace. The concept of eudemonia, expressed by Aristotle as happiness or human flourishing, is connected with UN documents articulating the need and actions necessary for a culture of peace. Aristotle's thinking about means and ends connects with the process orientation of contemporary peace educators other philosophical concepts within the virtue ethics frameworks come from Erasmus' humanism and Spinoza's disdain for war. Page suggests that the theological commitments of Dietrich Bonhoffer provide an example of moral courage. Some modern thinkers on virtue ethics and peace education include such prominent figures as Gandhi and Martin Luther King.

Peace education as a practice in schools is attributed to Maria Montessori, John Dewey and Paulo Freire, though earlier thought on education for peace is traced back to Erasmus and Socrates, among other scholars. Montessori worked to foster peace on three inter-related levels: the individual, community, and globe. The individual level relates to person-centered awareness of the self (*i.e.,* body, mind, emotions, and spirit), whereas the community level refers to interpersonal relations (*i.e.,* trust, openness, and interdependence), and the global level concerns cultural and environmental consciousness (Montessori 1949). Dewey informed peace education through his work on the relationship between education and democracy, stating that one role of education is to foster active citizenship through the participation in processes of democracy (Dewey 1916).

Freire (1970) centered education on revealing systems of oppression, particularly through the exploration of language and identity and by challenging the banking-model of teaching and learning. All three educators sought to create education that was learner-centered and autonomous. This concept of classroom education represents social outcomes relevant to democratic political systems. Hence, autonomous learning relates to individual and national autonomy and democratic classroom participation models active citizenship in a democracy. Peace education is also found philosophically in the work of authors (*e.g.,* Tolstoy, Thoreau), social thinkers (*e.g.*, Mead, Foucault, and Adams), social learning scholars (*e.g.,* Bandura and Walters) and activists (*e.g.*, Ghandi, King, Ikeda, Syuu Kyi).

In practice, peace education is problem-posing education that attempts to build in every person the universal values and behaviors on which a culture of peace is predicated, including the development of non-violent conflict resolution skills and a commitment to working together to realise a shared and preferred future. Many scholars in the field address violence and the war system as the core problematic inhibiting peace and seek to propose viable solutions to violence in all its manifestations (*e.g.,* social, economic, political, environmental, spiritual, and ethical). Violence might be defined as "avoidable, intentional harm, inflicted for a purpose or perceived advantage of the perpetrator or of those who, while not direct perpetrators, are, however, advantaged by the harm" (Reardon 2001, 35). Education for peace raises dialogue on critical issues at the heart of the community in order to transform oppressive systems from a violent orientation toward a culture of peace. Thus, through education for peace educators and students critically discuss manifestations of, and justifications for, violence, identify the actors involved and propose peaceful futures (Boulding 1988, Hicks 1994).

Peace education includes the cultivation of peace building skills (*e.g.,* dialogue, mediation, artistic endeavors).

Peace educators, then, teach the values of respect, under standing, and nonviolence, present skills for analysing international conflict, educate for alternative security systems, and use a pedagogy that is democratic and participatory. Thus, peace education as a practice and philosophy refers to matching complementary elements between education and society, where the social purposes (*i.e.,* why teach), content (*i.e.,* what to teach), and pedagogy (*i.e.,* how to teach) of the educative process are conducive to fostering peace. Accordingly, peace education is a dialogical experience conducted through participatory learning, where learners communally and co-operatively grapple with contemporary issues (*i.e.,* talking points) related to local and global contexts.

Classification of Peace – Positive and Negative Peace

Peace is sometimes equated with the absence of war. But think about a country today that is not at war. Would you describe that country as being peaceful? Are there still problems of physical violence? Are there issues of social inequality, injustice, or discrimination? Most likely, the answer is yes. These are the issues that renowned peace scholar Johan Galtung was trying to address when he developed the concepts of negative and positive peace.

Johan Galtung is one of the main theorists in peace and conflict studies. He introduced the concepts of negative peace, positive peace, structural violence, and many other key concepts. Galtung has written numerous books and journal publications, and is the founder of *Transcend International*, a network of organizations working in peace research, education, action and media. Galtung's ideas have been highly influential in the field of peace education.

John Galtung, the father of peace studies, refers to the distinction between 'Negative Peace' and 'Positive Peace' (Galtung 1964). Negative Peace refers to the absence of violence, it is negative because something undesirable stopped happening. Positive Peace is filled with positive content, and it's the integration of human society. Peace does not mean the total absence of any conflict. It means the absence of violence in all forms and the unfolding of conflict in a constructive way. Peace therefore exists where people are interacting non-violently and are managing their conflict positively – with respectful attention to the legitimate needs and interest of all concerned.

Positive peace is the presence of social justice and equality, and the absence of structural or indirect violence. It is characterized by the presence of harmonious social relations and the 'integration of human society' (Galtung, 1964). In order to further understand positive peace, it is important to understand structural violence.

Positive peace is more than the absence of violence; it is the presence of social justice through equal opportunity, a fair distribution of power and resources, equal protection and impartial enforcement of law.

Efforts to Achieve Positive Peace Emphasise

- Establishing peace through world order by supporting international law, compliance with multilateral treaties, use of international courts, and nonviolent resolution of disputes, participation in international organizations, trade, and communication.
- Establishing social equality and justice, economic equity, ecological balance; protecting citizens from attack, and meeting basic human needs.
- Establishing a civil peace that provides the constitutional and legal means necessary to settle differences non-violently.
- Eliminating indirect violence, that shortens the life span of people, sustains unequal life chances, or reduces quality of life for any citizen.
- Practicing conflict resolution as a foundation for building peaceful interpersonal and institutional relationships.

Positive peace refers to a "social condition in which exploitation is minimized or eliminated, and in which there is neither overt violence nor the more subtle phenomenon of underlying structural violence" (Barahs and Webel, 2002: 6). Positive peace focuses on peace building initiatives. It strives to establish social justice, and challenges conservative approaches and structures, by enhancing values of common well, economic and social equality, self-realisation and growth. This approach is mainly developed by the Norwegian scholar John Galtung who is considered to be one of the prominent researchers in the field of peace studies. Positive peace is a situation in which structural violence is eliminated, and as the contrary to the negative one, involve reconstruction of knowledge and the development of competences guided by the philosophy of a just society and the perusing of human rights. Martínez-Guzmán in his introduction to the chapter, Negative and Positive Peace talks about "we human beings have both the knowledge and the capacity to destroy ourselves [...] however human knowledge, capacity and competence demonstrate that there are many ways in which human beings can cultivate relationship" (Martínez-Guzmán, 2006: 23). The author suggests that in the same way humanity cultivate structural violence or negative peace; it can cultivate competences for non-violent relations, and ways of creating culture of peace. The two basic assumptions in this philosophy for peace are that human nature is intuitive and there for is competent and accountable for its action (Martínez-Guzmán, 2006: 24).

Negative Peace is the absence of violence. In order to create negative peace, we must look for ways to reduce and negative peace is the absence of direct violence (physical, verbal, and psychological) between individuals, groups, and governments.

Efforts to Achieve Negative Peace Emphasise

- Managing interpersonal and organizational conflict in order to control, contain, and reduce actual and potential violence.
- Reducing the incidence of war by eliminating the extreme dangers of the war system and limiting war through international crisis management.

- Preventing war through strategic deterrence and arms control.

The concept of 'Negative Peace' addresses immediate symptoms, the conditions of war, and the use and effects of force and weapons. Words and images that reveal the horror of war and its aftermath are often used by writers, artists, and citizen groups in their efforts to stop it imitate violence. A cease-fire would be an example of an action for negative peace.

Negative peace denotes the absence of war. It refers to a situation in which no active military violence is occurring. Both modern democracies, like: U.S., Israel Spain, and non-democratic states like: Iran, China or Morocco, are submitted to a situation of negative peace, in which they might not have an open declared war led by military reprisal, but are violating the rights of its people or others. According to international relation theories, peace is found where there is an absence of direct state violence (Bahsa and Webel, 2002: 1-27). In a more complex perception of the concepts of war, conflicts and peace, as Galtung suggests, the notion of violence contemplates not only a physical direct one (Bashar and Webel, 2002). He refers to the structural violence that is built into the proper structure of the social, cultural and economic dimensions of society.

Most peace promoters probably would agree that the most promising way to reduce negative relations to a minimum is via an increase of positive relations – but empirical correlation does not imply logical dependence, for which reason the two concepts should be kept separate. And which are these 'positive relations'?

Just to mention some examples:

1. Presence of co-operation.
2. Freedom from fear.
3. Freedom from want.
4. Economic growth and development.
5. Absence of exploitation.
6. Equality.

7. Justice.
8. Freedom of action.
9. Pluralism.
10. Dynamism.

All these values can be discussed at the intra-national level of individuals as well as at the international level of nations One can talk about individuals exploiting each other and nations exploiting each other, about individuals living in fear and anxiety and nations doing so, about individuals having a wide range of actions open to themselves so that they can live 'rich lives' and individuals that have a very narrow spectrum of actions from which they can choose, and one may talk about nations in the same way. Some comments of this set of ten values: By 'presence of cooperation' we mean a pattern of interaction between nations so that there is an exchange of values between them, of commodities, services, knowledge, people etc. This is the opposite of isolation, it is interdependence between nations.

By 'freedom from fear' we mean a state of affairs such that individuals, and nations, predict with relatively high probability a major negative event in the future, an event with relatively high negative utility, and this expectation dominates their life and existence – whether they live in the shadow of floods, earth-quakes, hunger, war (internal or external) or other calamities.

By 'freedom from want' we mean that neither in the life of the individuals nor in the life of the nations should major, primary needs remain unsatisfied or unsatisfiable. Thus, we mainly refer to such needs as: hunger, thirst, shelter, sex, basic security. By 'economic growth and development' we mean an organization of the structure of nations and the relations between nations so that:

1. Resources per capita increase.
2. These resources are better distributed. This is not only a question of technological development but also of social organization, at the national as well as at the international level.

By 'absence of exploitation' we mean that all value exchanges between individuals as well as between nations take place at, roughly, equal terms. Thus, no individual shall be able to receive very much more from another individual than he gives back to that individual (the example is, for instance, labour force in exchange for money), nor shall any nation be able to extract from another nation much more than she gives to that nation (the example here is, for instance, the rate at which raw materials are exchanged for industrial products in world trade).

By 'equality' we mean that all individuals and nations are regarded as having the same essential value, none is implicitly worth more and entitled to basically different types of life or existence than others. Extreme 'gaps' in opportunities and resources at the disposal of individuals or of nations should not be tolerated. By 'justice' one may mean roughly the same as by 'equality', but there is also the dimension of basic, fundamental rights, not only individual or national worth or value. By 'freedom of action' we mean that all individuals and nations should have a wide range of possible actions open to them - both that they have been stimulated to have the imagination to conceive of such action and that they have the means to carry them out. But the concept is problematic since it implies a kind of independence relative to other individuals or other nations that is incompatible with the interdependence. A person who is happily married renounces on certain types of freedom of action because he gains a wider range of possibilities – but whether the net gain is positive or negative may be a matter of debate. By 'Pluralism' we mean that nations and the world should contain a large social and cultural diversity of forms co-existing side by side, and by 'dynamism' we mean that at least parts of the nations and parts of the world are constructed in such a way that a change or conditions for a change are built into the structure. In other words, there must be options left open for future generations, policies that exclude too many options are harmful from that point of view.

Structural violence, or indirect violence, is the result of social structures or institutions that prevent people from meeting their basic needs and accessing their basic human rights. Assefa describes this as 'killing people without the use of the gun' (1993: 3). For example, hunger can be the result of structural violence, as economic and social systems may prevent people from being able to access adequate food supplies, particularly in societies where there are rich people with excess food supplies, and especially when public resources are diverted to other areas, such as military spending. Another example would be institutionalized racism or sexism.

Cultural violence refers to any aspect of culture which can be used to justify structural violence. Language, religion, ideology, and science are examples of parts of a culture that may mask structural violence, and even make it seem natural or right.

It is important to note that peace, whether negative or positive, does not necessarily mean the absence of conflict. Conflict itself is not an inherently negative occurrence, as through conflict, positive change and transformation may occur. What is important is that conflict is handled nonviolently and constructively. Turay and English (2008) express this idea clearly by saying, "conflict is a fact of life and a reality for all of us. How we deal with it is how we embody our understanding of peace and justice".

Peace education must distinguish between these different aspects of peace, and include both aspects in order to educate for a holistic conception of peace. In peace education, disarmament education and nonviolent conflict resolution education are forms of education for negative peace, as these forms of education seek to directly end or prevent violence and the use of force and weapons. However, disarmament education also goes beyond negative peace by promoting values for positive peace, and by exploring areas of structural violence relating to militarism, for example. Education for human rights, multiculturalism, social justice, ecological sustainability, and inner peace are examples of peace education for positive peace.

Assistance of Indian thought to Minimize the Negative Peace

Peace in Gandhian thought

Gandhi holds an important place in the history of social thought. Though he is not considered as a theoretician in strict sense yet his writings on state and democracy, relationship between individual and the society, moral and ethical values in education and numerous other writings on social issues have made him an invincible part of academic debates across political science, history, sociology, and economics among other subjects. This is very well reflected in Akeel Bilgrami's argument that "the social scientist's and historian's interest in him has sought out a nationalist leader with a strikingly effective method of non-violent political action" (Bilgrami, 2003: 4159). Additively, "he was basically a man of action whose major contribution consisted in leading his country's struggle for independence" (Parekh, 1997:151). The Gandhian thought of peace is worldwide acknowledged. The name of Gandhi is synonyms with peace and non-violence. That is why United Nation announced World Peace Day on 2nd October, the birth date of Mahatma Gandhi. The contribution of Gandhi to the humanity is incomparable. The present paper is an attempt to locate how he tended to blend peace education and education for peace within his broad schema on his ideas on education in general. Gandhi viewed education as vital in the overall development of individual as well as society. This education has to be given to the students so that they can learn and imbibe the ethics and values of a humanitarian, just and peaceful society *i.e.*, 'Sarvodya Samaj'.

Before elaborating on the Gandhian notion of peace education, we need to locate what peace education broadly means. Peace education can be understood education for facilitating peace. According to Page (2008) "a fundamental concern of peace education is education to prevent the suffering and wastage of warfare within the modern era" (Page, 2008: 2). Harris and Morrison (2003) argue that "peace education, refers to teaching about peace – what it is, why it doesn't exist, and how to achieve it" (Harris and Morrison, 2003: 25-26). According to Peace Education Working Group at UNICEF, peace education "refers to the process of promoting the knowledge, skills, attitudes and values....... to prevent conflict and violence." Hague Appeal for Peace defines peace education as "a participatory holistic process that includes teaching for and about democracy and human rights" among other issues.

For Gandhi, peace can be located in "his revolutionary mode of action which he called satyagraha, and his challenging goal of sarvodaya, meaning the welfare and good of all, a fuller and richer concept of people's democracy than any we have yet known' (Bose, 1981: 159). Peace to Gandhi is primarily located in his idea of Ahimsa *i.e.,* non-violence however, according to Gupta (1968: 1876), his ideas of trusteeship and passive resistance both form the base peaceful and just society. For Gandhi, "A votary of ahimsa...... remains true to his faith if the spring of all his actions is compassion, if he shuns to the best of his ability the destruction of the tiniest creature, tries to save it, and thus incessantly strives to be free from the deadly coil of himsa".

Gandhian concept of education is based on all round development of human personality that includes physical development, intellectual development and spiritual development. According to Gandhi, "By education I mean an all round drawing out of the best in child and man". Gandhi's important writing on education is compiled in two books; 'Basic Education' (1951) and 'Towards New Education' (1953). He didn't like the western education. According to him western education is based on materialism. In western philosophy the value of education is like the value of land or property, which is a very narrow concept. He believed that education is very broad concept and if it is implied in a better way, it can solve many problems of society and world.

Buniyadi Shiksha (Basic Education also known as 'Nai Talim') was the base of educational practice as propounded by Gandhi in 1937 at Wardha which subsequent became as Wardha Scheme or Basic National Education. As has been argued by Samuel Ravi, that "The principle of non-violence is the basis of basic education. Through it...... Gandhi wants to develop qualities which are necessary for building a non-violent society. It is against exploitation and centralization." (Ravi, 2011: 232). His idea of basic education was firmly oriented towards activity based. He elaborated on his notion of 'Nai Talim' as "Craft, Art, Health and education should all be integrated into one scheme. Nai Talim is a beautiful blend of all the four and covers the whole education of the individual from the time of conception to the moment of death".

The idea of sarvadharma samabhava *i.e.,* equality of religions as espoused by Gandhi is an effective tool to counter the increasing tensions among different religious groups. According to Gandhi, "a curriculum of religious instruction should include a study of the tenets of faiths other than one's own. For this purpose, the students should be trained to cultivate the habit of understanding and appreciating the doctrines of various great religions of the world in a spirit of reverence and broad-minded tolerance. This, if properly done, would help to give them a spiritual assurance and a better appreciation of their own religion. This study of other religions besides one's own will give one a grasp of the rock-bottom unity of all religions, and afford a glimpse also of that universal and absolute Truth which lies beyond the 'dust of creeds and faiths".

In some of the recent studies, scholars have tried to contextualize and place the emergence of Gandhian Studies within the framework of education for peace. Field (2006: 231) underlines that "non-violence education or Gandhian Studies emphasises positive concepts of peace (rather than peace as absence of strife)". Monisha Bajaj (2010: 47-63) in her study argues that "social and collective action towards peace also appears more frequently in Gandhian studies perhaps because of the focus on structural and cultural forms of violence" (Bajaj, 2010: 54). Similarly, Tint and Prasad (2007: 23-37) have also observed that "there are several programmes in Gandhian thought and peace studies, which inform the studies on nonviolence" (2007: 27). Thus, Gandhi emphasised on value education as it is necessary for moral development of individual whereas peace education is vital for humankind as a whole.

His idea of peace education can be seen in his interpretation of religious education though he was critical of it many a times. Religious education tends to sensitize individual towards his/her moral duties and responsibilities. All religions are based on love and compassion towards humanity and thus teach tolerance to its respective followers. Religious teachings should not be confused with the dogmatic, conservative and static notions of social reality rather these should be seen as a form of moral cleansing of individual. The practice of non-violence can achieve its optimum if one has an attitude of tolerance of others. He argued that religious and moral education in the overarching framework of non-violence is complimentary in nature and form the core of peace education. Peace education needs to inculcate tolerance among the different faiths. His thoughts on inequality, social development, education and non-violence if operationalised, can go a long way to negotiate and over come not only the socio-economic challenges but also the ethical dilemmas of present times.

Role of Different Organizations Like UNESO in Peace Enrichment

The United Nations was founded after the 'great and terrible' Second World War to create and maintain peace through economic, social or political agreements. But this is not enough. The foundations of peace still need to be laid, with the help of the specialized agencies which make up the United Nations system.

Since its foundation over 60 years ago, UNESCO took over that mission in conformity with its Constitution which asserts that, "since wars begin in the minds of men, it is in the minds of men that the defenses of peace must be constructed". In this regard, the same Constitution highlights that "a peace based exclusively upon the political and economic arrangements of governments would not be a peace which could secure the unanimous, lasting and sincere support of the peoples of the world, and that the peace must therefore be founded, if it is not to fail, upon the intellectual and moral solidarity of mankind". This mandate has gifted the Organization with a long standing experience in promoting mutual understanding while fighting discrimination, intolerance and violence.

An Everyday Peace Practice

The new global challenges and threats are multiplying and undermining social cohesion in a world where interdependence is growing and solidarity is diminishing. The constant question remains as to how we may best approach the unity-in-diversity way of life, or to learn how to 'live together' by fully participating in the infinite wealth of the cultures of the world and by averting the fear reflex when confronting with 'otherness'. As a consequence, greater account must be taken of the close links between cultural diversity, dialogue, development, security and peace. Thus, a genuine and lasting dialogue is imperative to rethink the benefits of cultural diversity for all and to bridge cultural and religious barriers as well as to break stereotypes and to turn people from violence.

Since words are the natural support to our thoughts, their use must mean something. In reality, which words should we choose to build, appropriate and extend this common aspiration of humankind, which draws upon its rich cultural diversity? It should be recalled that the United Nations, and UNESCO in particular, have always used the terms 'dialogue among civilizations', 'dialogue among cultures', 'rapprochement of cultures', 'tolerance' as well as 'culture of peace' to describe their conceptual, political and programmatic approach in suitable and convincing language.

Peace and Security

Saving succeeding generations from the scourge of war was the main motivation for creating the United Nations, whose founders lived through the devastation of two world wars. Since its creation, the UN has often been called upon to prevent disputes from escalating into war, or to help restore peace when armed conflict does break out, and to promote lasting peace in societies emerging from wars. The Security Council, the General Assembly and the Secretary-General all play major, complementary roles in fostering peace and security.

UN Peace and Security

Over the decades, the UN has helped to end numerous conflicts, often through actions of the Security Council – the organ with primary responsibility, under the United Nations Charter, for the maintenance of international peace and security. When a complaint concerning a threat to peace is brought before it, the Council's first action is usually to recommend to the parties to try to reach agreement by peaceful means. In some cases, the Council itself undertakes investigation and mediation. It may appoint special representatives or request the Secretary-General to do so or to use his good offices. It may set forth principles for a peaceful settlement.

When a dispute leads to fighting, the Council's first concern is to bring it to an end as soon as possible. On many occasions, the Council has issued ceasefire directives which have been instrumental in preventing wider hostilities. It also deploys United Nations peacekeeping operations to help reduce tensions in troubled areas keep opposing forces apart and create conditions for sustainable peace after settlements have been reached. The Council may decide on enforcement measures, economic sanctions (such as trade embargoes) or collective military action.

According to the Charter, the General Assembly can make recommendations on the general principles of co-operation for maintaining international peace and security, including disarmament, and for the peaceful settlement of any situation that might impair friendly relations among nations. The General Assembly can also discuss any question relating to international peace and security and make recommendations, if the issue is not currently being discussed by the Security Council.

Pursuant to its 'Uniting for Peace' resolution of November 1950 (resolution 377 (V), the General Assembly may also take action if the Security Council fails to act, owing to the negative vote of a Permanent Member, in a case where there appears to be a threat to or breach of the peace, or act of aggression. The Assembly can consider the matter immediately with a view to making recommendations to Members for collective measures to maintain or restore international peace and security.

Two of the General Assembly's six main committees are involved in matters of peace and security. Besides the First Committee which is concerned with disarmament and related international security questions, the Special Political and Decolonization Committee deals with a variety of political subjects not dealt with by the First Committee, including decolonization, Palestinian refugees, human rights, peacekeeping, mine action, outer space, public information, atomic radiation and the University for Peace.

The Charter empowers the Secretary-General to "bring to the attention of the Security Council any matter which in his opinion may threaten the maintenance of international peace and security". One of the most vital roles played by the Secretary-General is the use of his 'good offices' – steps taken publicly and in private that draw upon his independence, impartiality and integrity to prevent international disputes from arising, escalating or spreading.

Conflict Prevention

Conflict prevention remains one of the highest objectives of the United Nations. In today's world, preventive action extends well beyond traditional preventive diplomacy to involve a broad constellation of UN entities working across a wide range of disciplines – poverty eradication and development, human rights and the rule of law, elections and the building of democratic institutions and the control of small arms, to name just a few.

The Department of Political Affairs plays a central role in these efforts: monitoring and assessing global political developments; advising the UN Secretary-General on actions that could advance the cause of peace; providing support and guidance to UN peace envoys and political missions in the field; and serving Member States directly through electoral assistance and through the support of the work of the Security Council and other UN bodies.

Peacekeeping

The first UN peacekeeping mission was established in 1948, when the Security Council authorized the deployment of the United Nations Truce Supervision Organization (UNTSO) to the Middle East to monitor the Armistice Agreement between Israel and its Arab neighbors. Since then, there have been a total of 64 UN peacekeeping operations around the world.

Over the years, UN peacekeeping has evolved to meet the demands of different conflicts and a changing political landscape. Born at the time when the Cold War rivalries frequently paralyzed the Security Council, UN peacekeeping goals were primarily limited to maintaining ceasefires and stabilizing situations on the ground, so that efforts could be made at the political level to resolve the conflict by peaceful means.

UN peacemaking expanded in the 1990s, as the end of the Cold War created new opportunities to end civil wars through negotiated peace settlements. A large number of conflicts were brought to an end, either through direct UN mediation or by the efforts of others acting with UN support. Countries assisted included El Salvador, Guatemala,

Namibia, Cambodia, Mozambique, Tajikistan, Sierra Leone, and Burundi. As the decade drew to a close, continuing crises led to new operations in the Democratic Republic of the Congo, the Central African Republic, Timor Leste, Sierra Leone and Kosovo.

The nature of conflict has also changed over the years. Originally developed as a means of dealing with inter-State conflict, UN peacekeeping has been increasingly applied to intra-State conflicts and civil wars. Although the military remain the backbone of most peacekeeping operations, today's peacekeepers undertake a wide variety of complex tasks, from helping to build sustainable institutions of governance, through human rights monitoring and security sector reform, to the disarmament, demobilization and reintegration of former combatants, and demining.

The Department of Peacekeeping Operations (DPKO) provides political and executive direction to UN peacekeeping operations, and maintains contact with the Security Council, troop and financial contributors, and parties to the conflict in the implementation of Security Council mandates. The Department works to integrate the efforts of UN, governmental and non-governmental entities in the context of peacekeeping operations. DPKO also provides guidance and support on military, police, and mine action and other relevant issues to other UN political and peace building missions.

In 2007, DPKO was split up, with the establishment of the Department of Field Support (DFS), which provides dedicated support and guidance to peacekeeping and political field missions in the areas of finance and budget; personnel and human resources; logistics and information, communication and technology.

Peace Building

The experience of recent years has also led the United Nations to focus as never before on peacebuilding – efforts to reduce a country's risk of lapsing or relapsing into conflict by strengthening national capacities for conflict management, and to lay the foundations for sustainable peace and development.

Building lasting peace in war-torn societies is among the most daunting of challenges for global peace and security. Peacebuilding requires sustained international support for national efforts across the broadest range of activities – monitoring ceasefires; demobilizing and reintegrating combatants; assisting the return of refugees and displaced persons; helping organize and monitor elections of a new government; supporting justice and security sector reform; enhancing human rights protections and fostering reconciliation after past atrocities.

The United Nations has been at the centre of expanding international peacebuilding efforts, from the verification of peace agreements in Southern Africa, Central America and Cambodia in the 1990s, to subsequent efforts to consolidate peace and strengthen states in the Balkans, Timor-Leste, and West Africa, to contemporary operations in Afghanistan, Haiti and Sudan.

Recognising that the United Nations needs to better anticipate and respond to the challenges of peacebuilding, the 2005 World Summit approved the creation of a new Peacebuilding Commission. In the resolutions establishing the Peacebuilding Commission, resolution 60/180 and resolution 1645 (2005), the United Nations General Assembly and the Security Council mandated it to bring together all relevant actors to advise on the proposed integrated strategies for post conflict peacebuilding and recovery; to marshal resources and help ensure predictable financing for these activities; and to develop best practices in collaboration with political, security, humanitarian and development actors.

The resolutions also identify the need for the Commission to extend the period of international attention on post-conflict countries and where necessary, highlight any gaps which threaten to undermine peacebuilding. The General Assembly and Security Council resolutions establishing the Peacebuilding Commission also provided for the establishment of a Peacebuilding Fund and Peace building Support Office.

Women, Peace and Security

While women remain a minority of combatants and perpetrators of war, they increasingly suffer the greatest harm. In contemporary conflicts, as much as 90 per cent of casualties are among civilians, most of whom are women and children. Women in war-torn societies can face specific and devastating forms of sexual violence, which are sometimes deployed systematically to achieve military or political objectives. Moreover, women continue to be poorly represented in formal peace processes, although they contribute in many informal ways to conflict resolution.

However, the UN Security Council has recognised that including women and gender perspectives in decision-making can strengthen prospects for sustainable peace. This recognition was formalized in October 2000 with the unanimous adoption of resolution 1325 on women, peace and security. The landmark resolution specifically addresses the situation of women in armed conflict and calls for their participation at all levels of decision-making on conflict resolution and peace building.

Since the agenda was set with the core principles of resolution 1325, three supporting resolutions have been adopted by the Security Council — 1820, 1888 and 1889. The four resolutions focus on two key goals: strengthening women's participation in decision-making and ending sexual violence and impunity.

Culture of Peace and Sustainable Development

In the new, turbulent international globalised landscape, a central idea emerges: greater account must be taken of the close links between cultural diversity, dialogue, development, security and peace. One of the most crucial challenges for UNESCO is to rethink these five interdependent notions so as to inform new approaches in all domains. From that perspective, the culture of peace imposes itself as the main strategic focus of UNESCO, along with sustainable development, both of which form two sides of the same coin. Peace has often been seen and portrayed (see illustration) as being the essential condition of sustained prosperity and prosperity itself, when shared, as fostering peaceful environments. Today, sustainable development calls to rethink our relationship to the economy, to society and the environment, bearing in mind that the emerging and future challenges of humankind do require collective responses, which implies the kind of solidarity that can result only from a culture of peace, non-violence and dialogue which condenses 'that which binds' cultures and societies to each other and from within. In turn, a culture of peace fosters sustainable development since it is aimed at helping people cope resiliently and creatively with ethical, cultural, political, environmental and other social transformations.

The Need of a New Programme on Culture of Peace and Non-violence

In its essence, the culture of peace and non-violence is a commitment to peace-building, mediation, conflict prevention and resolution, peace education, education for non-violence, tolerance, acceptance, mutual respect, inter-cultural and interfaith dialogue and reconciliation. It is a conceptual as well as a normative framework envisaged to inspire thoughts and actions of everyone. Therefore, it requires cognitive as well as the emotional abilities to grapple with our own situation in a rapidly changing world as well as with the emerging world society. This aim entails not just more factual knowledge, but also the broadening of our consciousness and the willingness to develop a new awareness, a new way of being in this world, a new 'mental mapping'.

As stated by the UNESCO Director – General, "Peace is more than the absence of war, it is living together with our differences – of sex, race, language, religion or culture – while furthering universal respect for justice and human rights on which such coexistence depends". Therefore, peace should never be taken for granted. It is an on-going process, a long-term goal, which requires constant engineering, vigilance and active participation by all individuals. It is a choice to be made on each situation, an everyday life decision.

The culture of peace continuously brings new challenges prompting us to reconsider the fundamental principles of humanity by highlighting what binds cultures and societies to each other and from within. Since what unites us is deeper than what separates us, there is a true ethic of living together that is taking shape in the culture of peace and non-violence process.

With a View to Achieve the following Expectations

Fundamental principles of peace universally shared to be appropriated by different cultures, thanks to a genuine dialogue and mainstreamed into public policies; Tension between universality and particularism, cultural identities and citizenship in a globalised world analysed and better understood; Everyday Peace to be conceived as an everyday living experience, not only in periods of conflict, but also in ordinary times.

The New Programme of Action on Culture of Peace and Non-violence Implies two Essential Approaches:

1. To rethink the dividends of cultural diversity, as benefits of a continuous exchange between cultures.
2. To promote the principle of learning to live together, the challenging Art of Unity-in-Diversity conducive to a lasting conviviality.

Pursuing these three Main Goals:

(i) To develop a new political, conceptual and programmatic approach in favor of a strong commitment by States and civil society to nurture 'everyday peace' involving women and youth, (*i.e.*, through ICTs and social media).

(ii) To improve the world's global understanding and deconstruct preconceived ideas by placing emphasis on the future as a humanistic aspiration (*i.e.*, by establishing guidelines for a global curriculum on shared values).

(iii) To promote a global movement in favor of the ideals and practice of a culture of peace and non-violence with emphasis on youth civic engagement and democratic participation (*i.e.*, by creating 'hubs of peace').

Peacekeeping is defined by the UN Department of Peacekeeping Operations as an "activity aimed at conflict control, which involves a...presence in the field...to implement or monitor the implementation of arrangements relating to the control of conflicts (cease-fires, separation of forces, etc.), and their resolution (partial or comprehensive settlements) and/or to protect the delivery of humanitarian relief". In the case of factional conflict within a country, peacekeeping often takes the form of separating the enemy groups and ensuring the safety of civilians and other noncombatants. In the sphere of international combat, peacekeeping usually involves patrolling borders and otherwise monitoring the conditions of a ceasefire.

Historically, nations have maintained and employed their armed forces for the explicit purposes of defending themselves against aggression and pursuing wars of conquest. Consequently, armies have developed with the technology, command structure, and strategies necessary to fight and defeat other regular armies. Peacekeeping, however, is a radically different military venture: instead of simply defeating a foreign power that poses a threat to national security, armed forces must participate in a remarkably complex, often multinational undertaking aimed at preventing armed conflict and protecting civilians.

Both in the world and in every community, we need to have peace. All human beings share the same needs, and there are many ways that we can make our community peaceful and spread this around the world. We don't always need a big group to make a difference. The smallest groups can start making change and it can spread to others.

In his 1992 report, 'An Agenda for Peace,' former UN Secretary-General Boutros Boutros-Ghali introduced the concept of peacebuilding to the UN as "action to identify and support structures, which will tend to strengthen and solidify peace in order to avoid a relapse into conflict (paragraph 21)". Over the years, various efforts have been made to elaborate on this definition. The Brahimi Report from 2000 defined peacebuilding as "activities undertaken on the far side of conflict to reassemble the foundations of peace and provide the tools for building on those foundations something that is more than just the absence of war" (paragraph 13). The Secretary-General's Policy Committee has described peacebuilding as:

"A range of measures targeted to reduce the risk of lapsing or relapsing into conflict by strengthening national capacities at all levels for conflict management, and to lay the foundation for sustainable peace and development. Peacebuilding strategies must be coherent and tailored to the specific needs of the country concerned, based on national ownership, and should comprise a carefully prioritized, sequenced, and relatively narrow set of activities aimed at achieving the above objectives".

The Secretary-General has set out his vision for peacebuilding in three reports (A/63/881–S/2009/304, A/64/866–S/2010/386 and A/67/499-S/2012/746) on post-conflict peacebuilding, and one (A/65/354–S/2010/466) on women's participation in peacebuilding. The 2009 report identified five recurring priority areas for international assistance:

1. Support to basic safety and security.
2. Political processes.
3. Provision of basic services.
4. Restoration of core government functions.
5. Economic revitalization.

The report also laid out an accompanying agenda for action for the UN. The 2010 and 2012 reports detail the progress the UN has made against this agenda, as well as toward the Seven-Point Action Plan contained in the report on women's participation in peacebuilding.

The 2012 report states that the UN and its partners must do more to ensure that countries emerging from conflict are able to contain and manage conflict themselves and transform it into sustainable peace. The report identifies inclusivity, institution building and sustained international support, as critical actions in preventing relapse into violence and producing more resilient societies. The report also notes that successful peacebuilding processes must be transformative, creating space for a wider set of actors – including women, youth, marginalized groups, civil society, and the private sector – to participate in national post-conflict decision-making. With respect to institution building, the report observes that public administration and social services delivered equitably and accountably can help in addressing grievances and rebuilding a country's legitimacy.

The 2012 report reflects not only lessons learned from the UN's experience in peacebuilding, but also wider policy discussions that have taken place amongst peacebuilding stakeholders. Countries emerging from conflict together with development partners, the UN and other international organizations, have articulated a shared vision of peacebuilding through the International Dialogue on Peacebuilding and State-building. The New Deal for Engagement in Fragile States, a policy framework emanating from the Dialogue, identifies five overarching peacebuilding and state-building goals:

1. Legitimate (inclusive) politics.
2. People's security.
3. Access to justice.
4. Employment generation and livelihoods support.
5. Accountable revenue management and service delivery.

The New Deal emphasises the need to anchor support activities in nationally owned peacebuilding plans and endorses the use of compacts+ as a means to implement those plans. The PBF, within its Terms of Reference, contributes to the achievement of the Peacebuilding and State-building

Goals and aligns its current Priority Areas and sub-categories of engagements to New Deal principles if needed.

Within this general framework peace building programmes are strategic, prioritized interventions driven by the analysis of a conflict and addressing underlying causes and consequences. These programmes build confidence in peace agreements and transitional processes, and contribute to restoring social contracts and strengthening social cohesion. They may include activities that facilitate inclusive participation in political processes, dialogue and reconciliation or that strengthen access to justice and human security. They may also include peace dividends: tangible results of peace that are delivered ideally by the state, or are at least attributable to it, and are accessible to communities in an equitable manner. They also create incentives for non-violent behaviour, reduce fear amongst the general population and begin the process of instilling trust in institutions and the larger peace process. Public administration and social services, delivered in an effective and equitable manner, can address grievances that underlie or trigger violent conflict and offer a means for the state to reach out to society and rebuild its legitimacy and systems of accountability.

2

Values

Values

Values regulate and guide human behaviour and action in our day-to-daily life. Values are embedded in every word we select and speak, what we wear, ways in which we interact, our perceptions and interpretation of others reactions in what we are say and so on. Values are formed on the basis of interests, choices, needs, desires and preferences. These comprise the nuclei of value formation. Values have a selective or directional quality. When preferences acquire certain definiteness, intensity and stability, these become the criteria for judgment, choices, action and grounds for decision-making in behaviour. Value thus is considered to be an enduring belief upon which human beings act by preferences.

Values involve the processes of thinking, knowing/ understanding feelings and action. These involve feelings *i.e.,* strong liking for something, feeling deeply about the things one values and so on. People's action often gives us clues as to what they value. Values are learnt as we learn habits in the process of growing up. Learning of values takes place quite early in life by the word of mouth or simple commands from parents and other adults at home. In early years of life, prohibitions and parent identifications are the source of values.

Definitions of Human Value

(a) *Roketch*: Value is defined as enduring belief, a specific mode of conduct or end state of existence along with continuum of importance.

(b) *Kluchhohn*: Value is a conception of desirable and not something desired.

(c) *Shaver*: Values are standards and principles for judging worth.

(d) *Gawande*: It is an adjusted human behaviour which is conductive to the development of himself, society, nation and international understanding.

The Indian Constitution has explicitly laid down fundamental duties of its citizens in Article 51A, emphasising that every Indian citizen would:

- 'Promote harmony and spirit of common brotherhood, transcending religious, linguistic and regional or sectoral diversities.
- Renounce practices derogatory to the dignity of women.
- Value and preserve the rich heritage of our composite culture.
- Protect and improve the natural environment.
- Develop the scientific temper.
- Abjure violence.
- Strive towards excellence in all spheres of individual and collective activity so that the nation constantly rises to higher levels of endeavor and achievement'.

In its Preamble itself, the Constitution lays down four universal values:

(i) *Justice*, social, economic and political.

(ii) *Liberty* of thoughts, expression, belief, faith and worship.

(iii) *Equality* of status and of opportunity; and to promote among them all.

(iv) *Fraternity*, assuring the dignity of the individual and the unity and integrity of the nation.

Values are relatively stable beliefs about what is important and what ends should be sought. Values are generally consistent across various situations. Decision-making criteria and their relative weight in a decision-making process are a function of one's values. While attitudes are associated with people, products, organizations and other tangible things, values are desired end states. Values are essentially emotionally driven in that there is no empirically set standard as to what outcomes one should value. Without an affective system, an individual can determine through experience and research what particular paths are the most effective means of achieving an end state, but cannot determine what end state is more desirable. Values are the desirable ends, goals or modes of action which makes human behaviour selective. Value not only orients but also determines human behaviour.

Classification of Values

There is a number of classification schemes used to categorise values. Here are a few of them.

- *Terminal vs. Instrumental Values*: Terminal values are desired end states. They represent a position in life or society one desires to exist or achieve. When an individual can no long answer the question of 'why' with 'because...' a terminal value has been reached. Instrumental values are desired means to achieve these ends. They represent preferred patterns of behaviour.
- *Merit vs. Worth.* A similar distinction can be made between the two fundamental ways in which individuals access or attach value to things. The two methods of evaluating values are the assessments of merit and worth. Merit is intrinsic and context-free value. This is value in its own right, independent of

possible applications, utility, or uses. A scholar of Middle Eastern cultures and religions know as the preeminent expert in this field may be evaluated high in terms of merit despite the fact that her university has not programme or course utilising this expertise. Worth is extrinsic and context-determined value. This is value based on application or usefulness in solving a problem or accomplishment of a goal. The worth of the same scholar would increase as the demand to courses in this field increases to the point that the university feels compelled to offer them.

- *Private vs. Public Values:* Private values are often called internalized values or enacted values. These are the values individual actually hold and use in making-decision; especially those decisions of which others are not aware. I have heard these referred to as 'what people do in the dark'. Public values, or espoused values, are those values we wish others to believe we hold.
- *Personal vs. Social Values*: Personal values are unique to an individual and are a function of past experiences, developmental socialization and interaction with others. These are often referred to as internalized values. Social values are values espoused my members of a group (cultural values) or members of an organization (organizational values).

Values in Organizational Context

- *Motivation*: When thinking about motivation as a behavioural choice process, we most often turn to the Expectancy Theory of motivation. One of the three components of this model is the valance, or value, of the expected outcomes of a behavioural choice. An individual's value structure has very strong influence on the valance attached to various outcomes.
- *Decision-Making*: The decision-making process is composed of three components; *(i)* Criteria, *(ii)* alternatives, and *(iii)* cause and effect beliefs

(theories). The value structure of individuals influences the weight or importance of various criteria used to make decisions.

- *Conflict:* Conflict between individuals and groups is a function of either disagreement about theories or interests. The strength of or importance of a party's interests are a function of value structure.
- *Ethics*: Values, both private and public, play a central role in determining what behaviours and choices are viewed as ethical or unethical by members of a culture.
- *Socialization*: One of the roles of a socialization process in a group or organizations is to communicate its public values to new members. When the socialization process is most effective, the publicly stated values of the group or organization become internalized as private values of the individual.
- *Work-Life Balance*: Work-life conflict and attempts to achieve balance between one's work and other activities is essentially a conflict between what an individual values. The priority that employees place on work, family, social and personal time is a function of their value structures.

Role of Community, School and Family in the Development of Values

Role of Community

Education as a Tool for Social Development

Education is at the heart of reconciliation, reconstruction and nation building programmes. Is education not a tool to enhance the realisation of people's full potential? If this were the case, the act of plunging into education is an empowering process. It is an act of enhancing the capacity and ability of people to act in a manner that directly and indirectly benefits them, their environment and the rest of creation. This suggests a personal and national responsibility to seriously take part in the education enterprise. Communities or people have to take part in defining and shaping their education.

Education is a process by which man accumulates knowledge. Skills and values are passed on from one generation to another. Those values should be taught in our school life which will assure a good generation ahead.

The whole enterprise of education is extricably linked with the development of values. Devoid of the potential to nurture values, education losses its heart and soul. No one who attempts to depict the spirit of age in which we live can possibly overlook the importance of education for values. Peace and security are facing new challenges that could have negative implications if we do not address them positively. The malleable years of youth in schools are crucial. Whatever is learnt and imbibed will determine to how students would live out their lives in future. The concern about value degradation is not new to this era. Even before independence such concern were pronounced in policy documents. Policy makers and educators have all along seriously mediated on this concern and have been trying to discern the potential of schooling, pinning their hopes on education to fulfill the aspirations and expectations of the public and the society.

The Report of the University Education Commission (1962) noted, "If we exclude spiritual training in our institutions, we would be untrue to our whole historical development." The Report went on to make a case, not for religious or moral education, but for evolving "a national faith, a national way of life based on the Indian outlook on religion, free from dogmas, rituals and assertions." The Education Commission of 1964-66 put the spotlight on 'education and national development', from which perspective it identified the 'absence of provision for education in social, moral and spiritual values' as a serious defect in the curriculum. The Commission recommended that these values be taught "with the help, wherever possible, of the ethical teachings of great religions." Agreeing with the Sri Prakasa Committee Report, it recommended 'direct moral instruction' for which 'one or two periods a week should be set aside in the school time-table'.

The National Policy on Education (1986) expressed concern over "the erosion of essential values and an increasing cynicism in society". It advocated turning education into a "forceful tool for the cultivation of social and moral values." Education should "foster universal and eternal values, oriented towards the unity and integration of our people". The Programme of Action of 1992 tried to integrate the various components of value education into the curriculum at all stages of school education, including the secondary stage.

The Government of India's report on Value Based Education (Chavan's Committee Report, 1999) submitted in both houses of Parliament, provided impetus to resume work on value orientation of education. The National Curriculum Framework for School Education (2000), echoing the National Policy on Education (1986), lamented the "erosion of the essential, social, moral and spiritual values and an increase in cynicism at all levels." Against this backdrop, the frame work advanced a plea to integrate value education into the curriculum asserting that: "Schools can and must strive to resolve and sustain the universal and eternal values oriented towards the unity and integration of the people enabling them to realise the treasure within" (p.8). It further stated that the "the entire educational process has to be such that the boys and girls of this country are able to see good, love good and do good and grow into mutually tolerant citizens" (p.36).

The National Curriculum Framework, 2005 echoed the vision of education where values are inherent in every aspect of schooling. The framework articulates the need to reaffirm our commitment to the concept of equality amidst diversity, mutual interdependence of humans to promote values that foster peace, humaneness and tolerance in a multi cultural society (p.2). Enabling children to experience dignity, confidence to learn, development of self-esteem and ethics, need to cultivate children's creativity, making children sensitive to the environment and the need for fostering democracy as a way of life rather than only as a system of governance as well as the values enshrined in the Constitution assume significance in the framework. It further opines that independence of thought and action, capacity of value based decision-making, sensitivity to others' well-being and feelings should form the basis of rationale commitment to values.

The NCF, 2005 particularly emphasises Education for Peace as one of the national and global concerns. As the position paper on Education for Peace prepared by the National Focus Group as part of NCF, 2005 puts it, "Peace is contextually appropriate and pedagogical gainful point of coherence of values". Peace concretizes the purpose of values and motivates their internalization." Education for Peace has been considered as a strategy to make value education operative. It aims at equipping students with the values and attitudes required for living in harmony with oneself and others as responsible citizens.

3 Peace Education

Definition of Peace Education

Peace education is more effective and meaningful when it is adopted according to the social and cultural context and the needs of a country. It should be enriched by its cultural and spiritual values together with the universal human values. It should also be globally relevant. Peace education could be defined in many ways. There is no universally accepted definition as such. Here are some good definitions from peace literature.

A Peace education is an attempt to respond to problems of conflict and violence on scales ranging from the global and national to the local and personal. It is about exploring ways of creating more just and sustainable futures – R. D. Laing (I 978). Peace education is holistic. It embraces the physical, emotional, intellectual, and social growth of children within a frame work deeply rooted in traditional human values. It is based on philosophy that teaches love, compassion, trust, fairness, co-operation and reverence for the human family and all life on our beautiful planet – Fran Schmidt and Alice Friedman (1988).

Peace education is skill building. It empowers children to solve conflict and to live in harmony with themselves, others, and their world. Peace building is the task of every human being and the challenge of the human family – Fran Schmidt and Alice Friedman (1988).

The basic concepts embedded in the above definitions are that peace education is a remedial measure to protect children from falling into the ways of violence in society. It aims at the total development of the child. It tries to inculcate higher human and social values in the mind of the child. In essence it attempts to develop a set of behavioural skills necessary for peaceful living and peace-building from which the whole of humanity will benefit.

In fact, two out of the four pillars of education suggested by the Dolor report, namely: learning to live together and learning to be, are related to peaceful living. Naming such efforts as peace education is not always necessary. What matters is integrating peaceful attitudes, values, and skills into the teaching and learning process in school and makes it a part of the total curriculum. Certain countries and institutes have it in the form of subjects such as Values Education, (Malaysia and Philippines), Citizenship Education (U.S.A.). Education for Mutual Understanding (Ireland) and Developmental Education (UNICEF). Apart from such subject names it can be integrated into the formal curriculum and co-curriculum of schools. Through applying peace education and creating a peace culture, it has been observed that schools can have the following benefits (as reported by teachers and principals who have used the peace approach in their schools in Sri Lanka. *Source*: Education for Conflict Resolution Project, National Institute of Education. Sri Lanka).

Peace education brings together multiple traditions of pedagogy, theories of education, and international initiatives for the advancement of human development through learning. It is fundamentally dynamic, interdisciplinary, and multicultural and grows out of the work of educators such as John Dewey, Maria Montessori, Paulo Freire, Johan Galtung, Elise and Kenneth Boulding, and many others.

Building on principles and practices that have evolved over time, responding to different historical circumstances, peace education aims to cultivate the knowledge, skills, and attitudes needed to achieve and sustain a global culture of peace. Understanding and transforming violence is central. The following diagram helps visualize the core relationship between violence and peace.

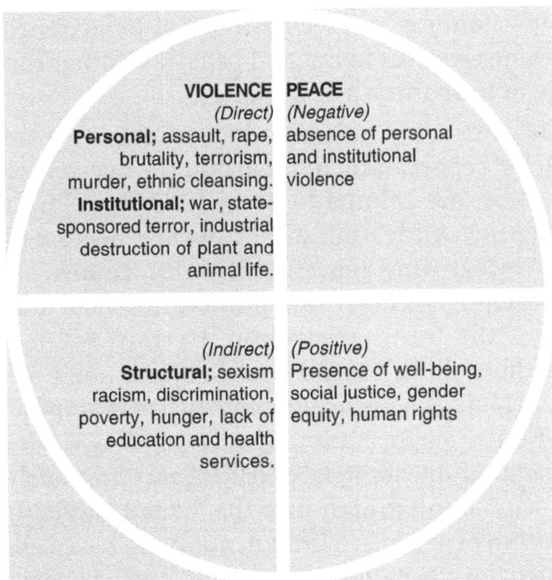

Peace is understood not only as the absence of traditional forms of direct violence, but also as a positive presence. Educating for and about all aspects of peace constitutes peace education.

Teaching of Peace Education

Peace education is a broad field and can be difficult to define. Very simply, peace education empowers learners with the knowledge, skills, attitudes and values necessary to end violence and injustice and promote a culture of peace.

Human Rights Education, Multicultural Education, Global Citizenship Education, and Conflict Resolution Education all fall under the scope of Peace Education and provide different approaches to the field. Although peace education is highly contextual and often tailored to specific settings or regions, the underlying goal is the same – peace is peace, no matter where you are.

SKILLS

Communication, Active Listening and reflection
Co-operation
Empathy and compassion Critical thinking and problem-solving
Artistic and aesthetic
Mediation, negotiation and conflict resolution
Patience and self-control
Responsible citizenship
Imagination
Leadership, vision

KNOWLEDGE

Self-awareness, recognition of prejudice
Issues relating to;
Conflict and war
Peace and non-violence
Environment/ecology
Nuclear and other weapons
Justice and power
Theories and conflict analysis, prevention, and resolution
Culture, race, gender, religion
Human Rights, responsibilities
Globalization
Labour
Poverty and international economy
International law and Criminal Court
United Nations, International system standards and instruments
Healthcare, AIDS
Drug trade

ATTITUDES

Ecological awareness
Self-respect
Tolerance
Respect for human dignity and difference
Intercultural understanding
Gender sensitivity
Caring and empathy
Non-violence and reconciliation
Social responsibility
Solidarity, world-mindedness
resolution

The diagram illustrates the relationships among the central knowledge, skills, and attitudes of peace education.

They are drawn from educational initiatives all over the world and form the basis of the learning objectives.

Scope of Peace Education

Peace education is an essential component of quality basic education. Peace education is the process of promoting the knowledge, skills, attitudes and values needed to bring about behaviour changes that will enable children, youth and adults to prevent conflict and violence, both overt and structural; to resolve conflict peacefully; and to create the conditions conducive to peace, whether at an intrapersonal, interpersonal, intergroup, national or international level. Peace education programmes have been developed in a number of UNICEF country offices and National Committees for UNICEF over the past decade. Ideasare continually evolves about how to use the full range of children's educational experiences to promote commitment to principles of peace and social justice.

Therefore, this paper should be seen as a working document, rather than a statement of policy. Its purpose is to stimulate further discussion and networking among UNICEF colleagues, to move towards a clearer articulation of good practice in peace education, and to pave the way for further exploration of how best to evaluate the impact and effectiveness of this area of UNICEF activity. As the need to evaluate peace education programmes becomes greater, so too does the need for a common framework within which to examine their content and methods and its relevance. In tracing the recent development of peace education, we begin to see that in the past it had been an integral part of education at all times and in all cultures, every culture regards peace as a noble ideal to attain. However with the advent of Western secularism at the beginning of the 20th century through the guise of a positivist scientific outlook to education, moral and human values including peace were slowly discouraged away from school curricula. Under the ideal of value-free positivist and reductionist knowledge the whole education was viewed narrowly as teaching facts of various subjects.

However, in spite of such materialistic views, the thinking of such humanists like: Rousseau, Henry Thoreau, Tolstoy and Maria Montessori kept the sense of education alive. With the witness of the horrors of the First and Second World Wars there was a reawakening to the need of developing the humanistic side of education at least among a few educationists. In this context Maria Montessori's loud and tireless reiteration on the need for educating for peace should be mentioned here with respect and appreciation. At the beginning of the 21st century today we are only rediscovering her vision of peace education which she tried to tell the world in the 1930s. For instance, she said in one of her public talks: Those who want war prepare young people for war; but those, who want peace have neglected young children and adolescents so that they are unable to organize them for peace.

Her vision of education provides a meaningful sound basis for peace education. She looked at education as a tool for building World Peace. To her peace is the guiding principle of man and nature. Any attempt to deviate from the principle will only bring about destruction. However it has never been investigated seriously so far. Peace should be studied as a science identifying its direct and indirect complex factors. She also observed that man had neglected to realise his inner sources of energies. Mastery over the external world alone is inadequate in bringing about a peaceful world. Peace is not only cessation of war. There are many positive qualities in peace. She said that violence destroys the moral perception inherited in man. She described her time as an era of insidious madness, which demanded man to return to reason immediately. Like Rousseau, she believed that man is intrinsically pure by nature. The child's natural innocence has to be preserved from being sidetracked or spoilt by society. To her the child is the promise of mankind. The child has real vision, a bright little flame of enlightenment that brings us a gift. Constructive education for peace must aim to reform humanity so as to permit the inner development of human personality and develop a more conscious vision of the mission of mankind and the present conditions of social life. What we need today is an education that is capable of saving mankind from the present predicament. Such an education involves the spiritual development of man and the enhancement of his value as an individual and prepares the young people to understand the time in which they live. At school we must construct an environment in which children can be actively engaged in learning. Peace Education does not teach students what to think, but rather how to think critically. In the process, its holistic and participatory approach may conflict with more traditional curriculum design or strict standards-based schooling. Peace education aims not to reproduce but to transform. It consists of people "consciously striving to educate their successors not for the existing state of affairs but so as to make possible a future better humanity." (John Dewey, Democracy and Education) and with this task come significant challenges and opportunities for all involved.

One way to meet the challenges of peace education is to build bridges of support among key participants. Just as learning takes place in a broader social context and not exclusively in schools or classrooms, so peace education relies on families, communities, and social networks to affect positive and lasting change. The notion 'think globally, act locally' is central to educating for a culture of peace in that it links theory with practice, international issues to individual efforts. As a peace educator, you need not work alone. The international peace education community is active and growing through networks, publications, global campaigns, national initiatives, and international programmes. Concerned citizens, educators and activists of all ages around the world are promoting and building peace through education.

Need of Peace Education

In present scenario where we live, the society values material gains and profits above all. It is not an exaggeration if to say that in this materialistic era of science and technology, everything except morality has reached to its echelon. Values unlike other aspects have gone into abysses where human existence and its future looks dismal and in dark. Though every nation is worried about the continuous corrosion of values yet no serious action has been taken by any of the nations for the restoration of values. Even our current system of education is oriented towards giving knowledge and skills that would make students saleable products and nothing else. This education system has developed only cognitive aspect of a man and left effective and psychomotor aspects starving, which results in sordid rapes, heinous murders, treacheries, chicaneries, frauds and malpractices.

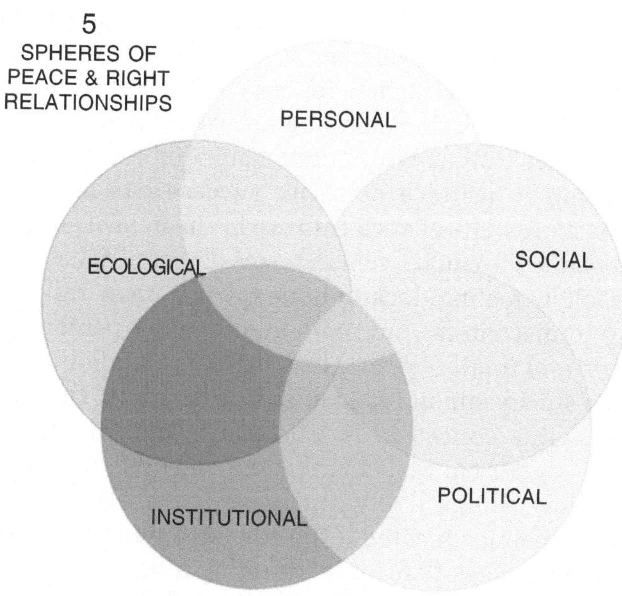

Such a system of education is devoid of the primary human values of solidarity, justice, equality, brotherhood, affection, generosity, empathy etc. Thus the problem of value crises seems to be inherent in the system of education itself. In the process of our gradual journey from primary to higher education two sorts of major changes, relative to our attitude towards values, occur in our life. They are external or bodily and internal or self-affirming. External changes in the sense that the students bag degrees by fair or foul means and on that basis get higher job positions. During the job, they collect more and more money, Cars, Bungalows and manage academic awards and all that by having which they may exploit themselves and the society with the disguised repute but they fears to face the deep hollowness of their disguised selves. They ruin self to the extent of dissatisfied and meaningless life. In brief, the more they adopt the disguise premises of life, which are ultra virus in higher education, the more their leadership in system is fixed but in the same proportion they find deconstruction of self-affirming values. Higher Education in the present era of LPG is stimulated by economic consideration without any reference to age old human values that separate man from animals. Cut throat competition to achieve material success has made man mechanical. Results of such rat race in the field of education and economic life can be seen in terms of insecurity, distrust, lack of fellow feeling, lack of honour for human values etc. leading to discontent and maladjustment in personal and social life and finally leading to drug abuse, maladjustment and even suicide among students. It is here that the urgent need for value education is felt by one and all currently. Values in higher education make one's own life and the life of his fellow beings lively and meaningful. Is there any meaning of being educated if the educated man is still away from getting a way of life and redeeming from the disastrous and life-killing ideologies? The purpose of education is self-affirmation and not self-negation. It is the process of removing the self-negating ideologies in order of self-affirmation. Peace education alone can provide real meaning and content in life.

Methods for Peace Education

Principles

Peace education methods are not arbitrary, but are based upon the following seven principles: Exemplary learning: the complexity of reality is reduced by identifying and addressing the varied linkages within a difficult issue area, which are often not immediately obvious.

- *Contrasting and Emphasising*: Methods focus attention on specific or determining view points and problematical aspects.
- *Change of Perspective*: Empathy is promoted by expanding the learners' own stand point, which can be inflexible and deeply rooted, to allow a plurality of views.
- *Clarity and Ability to Perceive Linkages*: using techniques such as visualisation, problematical issues are relocated from the realm of the abstract and related to learners' own, concrete experiences.
- *Action-orientated*: Themes and issues are made accessible through activity and experience – based learning.
- *Peer-orientated*: Shared learning is encouraged by group work and mutual support.
- *Empowerment*: Building skills promotes self-confidence and autonomy.

Peace Theory

The contested nature of 'peace' as a concept is demonstrated by the description of peace studies in the opening paragraph. Peace studies is defined in negative terms, by the central problems with which it is concerned: war, armed conflict and political violence. By implication, peace itself is understood primarily or initially as a negative, or as the absence of these phenomena.

It is this characterisation of peace as a negative phenomenon that prompted Johan Galtung to make his famous distinction between negative and positive peace in his article 'Violence, Peace and Peace Research' (1969). This distinction has since entered the lexicon of peace researchers and peace activists.

'Negative peace' is negative not because it is an undesirable goal, but because it is characterised by the absence or lack of these destructive social and political phenomena. 'Positive peace', on the other hand, is characterised by the presence of positive social and political phenomena such as justice, human rights, equality and well-being. Furthermore, it is suggested that positive peace provides the essential conditions of negative peace, because war, armed conflict and political violence result from the absence of positive peace. According to Ian Harris, '*Positive* peace is a condition where non-violence, ecological sustainability and social justice remove the causes of violence' (Harris, 2004:12).

This distinction between negative peace and positive peace did not originate with Galtung. Martin Luther King, for example, also employed it and said that: 'True peace is not merely the absence of some negative force – tension, confusion or war; it is the presence of some positive force – justice, good will and brotherhood' (King, 1957).

The Secondary Education Commission 1952-53 laid special emphasis on the following values in the formation of character of the students:

1. Efficiency.
2. Integrity.
3. Discipline.
4. Co-operation.
5. Good Temper.

The Committee of Religious and Moral Instruction headed by Shri Prakash made a special mention of dignity of labour, love of humanity, patriotism and self-discipline. Moral values particularly refer, to the conduct of man towards man in various situations good manners.

The Committee of Emotional Integration referred to the mutual appreciation of the various religions in the country spiritual values, national unity and the unity of mankind. The Education Commission emphasised the inculcation of the values of co-operation and mutual regard, honesty and integrity, discipline and social responsibility. It also stressed the development of scientific temper of mind, respect for manual labour, capacity to put in hard and responsible work, respect for an proper pride in the past faith and confidence in the future, national consciousness, spirit of social service for promoting social and national integration, equally essentials are values which help to make democracy a way of life and thereby strengthen it as a form of government, readiness to appreciate other's point of view and patience.

Ongoing Researches in the Field of Peace Education, Present Scenario and Suggestions

Education plays a vital role in equipping the nations in being more humane. The world is filled with trials and tribulations. Peace education only can extend a real peace in thus world. It has been said that if we are to reach real peace in this world we shall have to begin with the children. Not only some children but some adolescents and adults think that peace is not just the absence of war; it is the practice of love. In a peaceful society people would work together to resolve conflicts, develop morally, treat each other with justice, satisfy basic needs, and respect each other. In essence, they would live in unity. Our aim is not to achieve a perfect world. What we do want is much more unity and peace throughout the world. It has been found that there is no happiness greater than peace and that peace links with the practice of love.

Peace can take place within the individual. Some believe this inner peace can be strengthened through our relationship with the Divine. Inner peace involves peace of mind and absence of fear. Outer peace is peace in society. Our impression is that in India there is, in general, a greater stress on inner peace than in the West, where there is more

emphasis on outer peace. East and West must come together, as the world needs both. This is known as holistic inner-outer peace. It has both spiritual and material dimensions. The sacred texts of the world's great religions can help us better understand holistic inner-outer peace. Peace education would not exist unless people throughout the world believed that world peace is attainable through a multifaceted effort but starting with the education of children and youth. One such was Maria Montessori. Peace education is strengthened through the will-power and efforts of those who actively promote it, for they are aware of the terrible consequences if they do not. The horrors and suffering within our society and worldwide can be reduced if we have the strong will to act. In the words of the Indian thinker and philosopher Sarvepalli Radhakrishnan "We must will peace with our whole body and soul, our feelings and instincts, our flesh and its affections".

Achieving a culture of peace requires developing peaceful people. Peace education, broadly defined, includes all efforts to facilitate development of peaceful people. Peace education often takes place in schools, churches, families, community learning centres, counseling centres, clinics, prisons, and the workplace. Of course, it may occur anywhere, and the learners may be anyone – including young children, graduate students, United Nations peacekeepers, and police officers.

Harris (1999) delineated five types of peace education and described examples, goals, and content for each. 'Global peace education' includes international studies, holocaust studies, and nuclear education. 'Conflict resolution programmes' teach about mediation, negotiation, and communication skills. 'Violence prevention programmes' emphasise domestic violence, drug abuse, anger management, and teaching tolerance. "Development education" includes human rights education, environmental studies, and an emphasis on power and resource inequities and structural violence. 'Non-violence education' is based on the ideas of Gandhi, King, and other great peace-makers.

The essential content of peace education varies with time, place, and the particular needs of individuals, groups, and societies. Salomon (2002) has described how the challenges, goals, and methods of peace education differ substantially between areas characterised by intractable conflict, interethnic tension, or relative tranquility. Nevertheless, because some needs are common among people everywhere, certain elements of peace education may be seen as more universally essential.

In the 1980s nuclear war education was essential because of the nuclear arms race and the threat of nuclear holocaust. The continuing proliferation of nuclear and other weapons of mass destruction (WMD) and the possibility that terrorist groups might obtain WMD suggests that knowledge about threats of WMD should be considered an essential component of peace education for youth and adults throughout the world.

Attitudes, concepts, and competencies that generalize across all levels of conflict resolution from interpersonal to international and that may relate even to intrapersonal conflict, would seem to be particularly important as educational objectives. Democratic and tolerant attitudes, concepts like interdependency and reciprocity, and competencies for empathy, impulse control, problem-solving, and negotiation are examples of peace education objectives that are relevant for all levels of conflict.

One approach to defining the essential content of peace education assumes that its primary objective is to develop dispositions within people that will influence them to behave peacefully (Nelson and Christie, 1995). As elaborated by Staub (2002), the aims of peace education are to develop caring and non-aggressive individuals who relate peacefully to others in their own lives, who promote the welfare of others, and who take action to prevent violence in their society and in the world. Perhaps the most important contribution of psychology for peace education is to identify those dispositions – knowledge, competencies, attitudes, and values – that most strongly influence individuals' peaceful behaviour.

Another application of psychology to peace education provides guidance for selecting teaching methods and for creating a school climate conducive for learning. Research on teaching and learning has shown that students generally learn more when they are active, as when participating in group activities, engaging in role-plays, or working on projects. Students also 'learn by doing' when they serve as peer mediators. Co-operative learning, constructive controversy, and service learning have been shown to promote peaceful attitudes and competencies. Students are more likely to enjoy and to participate in classroom activities that are co-operative, democratic, and inclusive. One way to promote a democratic climate is 'negotiated learning' where students play a role in deciding what to study, how to study, and how to be evaluated.

Finally, a psychological approach to peace education emphasises the importance of scientific methodology in the evaluation of peace education methods and programmes. Current levels of violence and the threat of weapons of mass destruction pose an urgent need for effective peace education programmes. Scientific methods of evaluation are essential to discriminate between programmes that work and programmes that don't work. Schools, communities, and governments are not likely to adopt and sustain peace education programmes in the absence of sound evidence concerning their effectiveness.

International Peace Research Association, Australia has constituted Peace Education Commission and many ongoing researches are in vogue by this PEC. Werner Wintersteiner Centre of Peace Research and Peace Education, Klagenfurt University, Austria has its ongoing researches on "Global Citizenship Education – a Timely Term for Peace Education".

Principles of Peace Education

Peace education methods are not arbitrary, but are based upon the following seven principles:

1. *Exemplary Learning*: The complexity of reality is reduced by identifying and addressing the varied linkages within a difficult issue area, which are often not immediately obvious.
2. *Contrasting and Emphasising*: Methods focus attention on specific or determining viewpoints and problematical aspects.
3. *Change of Perspective*: Empathy is promoted by expanding the learners' own standpoint, which can be inflexible and deeply rooted, to allow a plurality of views.
4. *Clarity and Ability to Perceive Linkages*: using techniques such as visualization, problematical issues are relocated from the realm of the abstract and related to learners' own, concrete experiences.
5. Action-orientated: themes and issues are made accessible through activity and experience – based learning.
6. *Peer-orientated*: Shared learning is encouraged by group work and mutual support.
7. *Empowerment*: Building skills promotes self-confidence and autonomy.

The growth and development of peace studies requires strengthening or deepening its theoretical and conceptual framework and ensuring its relevance to effective action around the specific problems of war, armed conflict and political violence that are its core concerns. Both tasks can be accomplished, at least in part, through acknowledging (rather than suppressing) the explicitly normative or ethical dimension of peace studies, through the goals or objectives connected to peace activism and the role of human agency in achieving positive or beneficial social and political change. The example of Paulo Freire shows that peace education (like development education) plays a crucial role in providing an awareness of the transformative potential of human agency in achieving such change at multiple levels through critical, normative engagement with the social and conceptual worlds in which we live.

4

Value Education

Meaning of Value Education

Values education is activity which can take place in any organization during which people are assisted by others, who may be older, in authority or more experienced, to make explicit those values underlying their own behaviour, to assess the effectiveness of these values and associated behaviour for their own and others' long-term well-being and to reflect on and acquire other values and behaviour which they recognise as being more effective for long-term well-being of self and others.

Values education is an idea whose time has come and we're going to be hearing a lot more about it. Many politicians, social commentators and educationists believe that youth crime and misbehaviour are due to a loss of values and that giving youngsters values and a return to traditional/family values is the answer. But what a minefield! How can youngsters be given values? What are traditional values? What do we mean by 'family'? Is youth crime really due to a loss of values or to youth acting according to other kinds of values? Let's see what some of the terms in that definition mean.

Concept of Value Education

Value Education, as it is generally used, refers to a wide gamut of learning and activities ranging from training in physical health, mental hygiene, etiquette and manners, appropriate social behaviour, civic rights and duties to aesthetic and even religious training. To some, value education is simply a matter of developing appropriate behaviour and habits involving inculcation of certain virtues and habits. In opposition to such a conception, it is pointed out that value education has an essentially cognitive component in it and that this should not be ignored. Actually the ability to make moral judgement based on sound reasoning is a very important aim of value education and has to be deliberately cultivated.

Moral development of a child, according to some, results automatically from the social life of the school. The child as a member of the group imbibes the attitudes, values and general behaviour of the group and continually tries to mould himself according to the group norm. Such adjustment to life constitutes his moral development. Value Education is a process of aiding the child in such adjustment. Such a view is contested on the ground that although children learn the rules of group living from the social life of the school, such learning does not constitute value education. For morality, it is pointed out, is not concerned so much with 'what is' as with 'what ought to be' and 'what ought to be done'.

Value Education, according to one more view, is essentially a matter of educating the feelings and emotions. It is the 'training of the heart' and consists in developing the right feelings and emotions. It does not involve any cognitive abilities that can be trained. Like poetry, it is 'caught' rather than taught. It is essentially a matter of creating the right atmosphere, imitation and learning by example communion with nature or modeling one self after an ideal. Such a view is countered by saying that mere imitation of a 'good' person and modeling oneself after an ideal does not confer any morality on an individual.

Objectives of Value Education

Educational objectives refer to explicit formulations of the ways in which students are expected to be changed by the educative process. That is, the ways in which they will change in their thinking, their feelings and their actions. Objectives whether of value education or of any other curricular area depend on a variety of factors, psychological, sociological, epistemological.

Objectives of Value Education in the Modern Context

Objectives, especially in value education, have a temporal dimension. Traditionally the objectives of value education were based on religion and philosophy. There was no secular value education and very little scope for the development of moral thinking and the capacity for independent moral decision. In the modern world these are varieties of social demands made on the people. A civilized individual must possess certain minimum social skills. He has to establish decent relationship with people with whom he may come across for a short while or for a long duration. He may have to transact business in his private or public capacity. He has to function as a citizen of his state, or his country and of the world, all at the same time playing appropriate roles in each of these contexts. There are also many other demands made on him that need not be enumerated. Value education should therefore, it is pointed out, prepare an individual to meet these demands. That these cannot be accomplished in the form of a few do's and don't of the traditional form is quite evident. The Working Group on value oriented education has identified five dimensions on value education, these being physical education, emotional education, mental development, aesthetic development and the moral and spiritual domain. The values to be pursued in the moral and spiritual realm, according to them are:

Sincerity, faithfulness, obedience to what one conceives to be the highest, gratitude, honesty, benevolence, generosity, cheerfulness, self-lessness, freedom from egoism, equanimity in joy and suffering, in honour and dishonour, success and failure, pursuit of the deepest and the highest of the absolute and ultimate and the progressive expression of this pursuit in thought, feeling and action.

In many countries today the emphasis is on socio-economic reconstruction with the declared intention of a more equitable distribution of the benefits brought about by modernisation. Traditional cultural values have had little time to adjust to certain attributes of modernisation. Planners of value education curriculum then are faced with the problems of identifying values and character traits that will best equip the individual to take to his place in modern society. The objectives of value education should be such that the curriculum should recognise the tensions that are brought about by the conflicts between tradition and change. The planned programme should aim at developing a critical value perspective in our pupils that will enable them to employ modern skills for the betterment of mankind while helping them renew their commitment to fundamental traditional values.

Primary Moral Traits

1. To make right moral judgements.
2. To postpone gratification of desires.
3. To treat other human beings with dignity.
4. To be flexible in making moral judgements.
5. To be creative and dynamic in moral decisions.

Primary Moral Attitudes

The individual must be educated to possess the following attitudes:

1. *Autonomy:* Freedom of the will feel free to take a decision.
2. *Rationality:* Moral decisions based on reason.
3. *Altruism:* Extending help and cooperation to others self-sacrifice.
4. *Responsibility:* Prepared to own responsibility for all his actions accept guilt in all humility.

Scope of Value Education

The extent of well-being in any community depends on people's behaviour towards one and other. Values education is ultimately about changing behaviour for the better – to enhance well-being of all. It is surprising how many educators do not accept that their fundamental task is to change behaviour – even if this means encouraging deeper thinking or the correct use of chemistry apparatus. Educators who promote values education see it as a direct and effective contribution to reducing youth crime, drug misuse, vandalism, bullying, unwanted teenage pregnancy and so on. Of course, it is one's motives and how one does it that will determine the rightness or wrongness of attempts to change behaviour.

Values education does not dictate rules, promote lists of values or state desirable ways of behaving. Values education requires a new way of thinking about how to get youngsters to realise right from wrong. During values education the youngsters themselves decide what 'better' behaviour means. Instead of asking them to depend on some external code for judging the appropriateness of their behaviour, values education attempts to assist youngsters in building their own internal code. Motivated only by total concern and love (agape), the values educator, genuinely wants to know what youngsters think they should do in a moral dilemma or what they understand the values of 'respect' and 'honesty' entail in differing situations. Values educators attempt to participate as equals in these discussions – their views are one contribution, not the right answer.

Does this mean that we must do away with school rules? Not at all! If two children are involved in fisticuffs, the adult's duty is to impose his/her will and stop the fighting and state without consideration of the children's views, that fighting is unacceptable in school. However, this alone is not values education. Values education, through detailed and supportive discussion, should enable youngsters to reach the very bed-rock of what it means to be human and to make explicit for themselves the values they should act on to enhance their feelings of worth and meaningfulness.

This is why values education emphasises long-term well-being. Shoplifting might enhance the well-being of the thieves in the short-term. But in the long-term, well-being is diminished by the thief's dread of being caught, ostracised, and feelings of worthlessness and meaninglessness. Does this mean that values education is about social manipulation and conformity? No! Values education should give youngsters the rationale and courage to resist social norms or laws in the very rare instances when these blatantly infringe human dignity such as in slavery, the Nazi's treatment of Jewish people in World War II and apartheid. Values education transcends cultural and religious differences. How can values education be done?

In the context of schooling, values education can be undertaken by at least four main interrelated approaches:

1. The cross-curricular or permeation approach in which subject specialists identify values issues in, for example, history, geography or chemistry, and discuss them briefly when they arise during teaching.
2. The hidden curriculum that entails values educators attempting to become more aware of their behaviour and choosing only those behaviours they wish students to adopt. For example, the chemistry teacher would show respect for method, honesty in recording data and concern about the social implications of chemical products. Despite their status or educational attainments, values educators would attempt to regard all others (including cleaning and catering staff) as having equal worth as human beings.
3. The whole school ethos approach in which senior personnel take the initiative to implement organizational policies which entail the whole school in making explicit the values it stands for. Events and occasions would be organized whereby youngsters would have the

opportunities to act according to the values identified. This approach involves, for example, senior staff consulting teachers, students, janitorial staff and parents on how the school is to be administered. Within statutory guidelines teachers would consult with students on what and how they are taught; what school and classroom rules should be, and how rules should be monitored and rule-breakers treated.

4. The subject approach. A specific time could be set aside for group reflection and detailed discussions on the meaning of particular values, values issues and current social problems. Of course there will be some debate on what to call such a subject, but 'values education' is a sensible starting name. Values education is not necessarily the same as moral education, religious education, and personal and social education but an essential part of them.

Relevance of Value Education

Values shape our relationships, our behaviours, our choices, and our sense of who we are. The more positive our values, the most positive our actions. This is one of the reasons why values education is being taught or included in both elementary and Secondary levels because it plays a great role for students' becoming successful in their own choice of careers. It is the foundation of a morally upright person. The student of today is concerned with acquiring wealth, strength and position, but not good qualities. Education is meant to enable one to acquire what are good qualities. Education is not intended merely to stuff the brain with information. It has to transform the heart and make it pure. This sacred truth has been forgotten. When we have exemplary parents, exemplary leaders and ideal teachers, students will be ideal students, who are selfless, pure-hearted and innocent by nature, are being dragged into politics, their minds are getting fill with bitterness and hatred and their hearts are getting polluted.

Society can make human being as it want. But our present society is suffering with corruption in all the field due to our education system, because absence of value based education. Only one field has an important role to reduce all types of corruptions from the society is education. In this sense Value Based Education has an important role to make a new education system which will be based on the value. Because the element of Value Based Education can be found not only in the subject matter but in the learning styles which are employed, the scheduling of the classroom, extracurricular activities, and parental involvement. The value based education therefore organized so as to secure the fullest possible development of body, mind and heart; and a fruitful canalization of the life energy in pursuit that contribute to the growth of internal and external personality.

If human values take root in the educational system, the emerging individuals will have the following attributes:

- They will want peace and justice in a world that acknowledges the rule of law and in which no nation or individual need live in fear.
- Freedom and self-reliance to be available to all.
- The dignity and work of every person to be recognised and safeguarded.
- All people to be given an opportunity to achieve their best in life.
- They will seek equality before the law and the equality of opportunity for all.

Value Education, Fundamental Right, Duty and Role of Teacher

Value education is woven into the totality of educational programme in schools where value education does not form a mere appendage of all other subjects but would stand out as over-arching concern of basic importance. The books that students read, the school activities that are favoured or not favoured, the methods of teaching that are used by teachers, the role supervisors, teachers and pupils are expected to play in the maintenance of the rules and regulations of school, the manner in which particular events are celebrated and are chosen to exemplify their significance, the methods of evaluation, promotion, the way teachers are treated, the amount of freedom/initiative they enjoy, the kind of people serving on the school board and the way administrative staff functions is monitored etc., reflect and symbolize values.

The school atmosphere is surcharged with positive values to imbibe and internalize. Every teacher is a teacher of values. Teachers are properly oriented to create such environment for children where those values become vibrant. Their role is to put the child on the right path not by imposing but by watching, suggesting, helping. Each unit of study in the textbook for different subjects is related to value concerns through exercises, examples and question/discussion etc., as far as possible. Values permeate the formal curriculum as well as hidden curriculum and the pedagogical approach.

Parents are the child's first teachers and educators. Family is the first social unit where values begin to form and internalized, where DEPFE, NCERT fundamental needs of love, trust, care, belongingness, connections, autonomy and initiative during early years of childhood build the foundation for values. If parents do not care about the values that their wards will develop, these will remain incidental during the process of socialization. The concern for parents involvement in schools seems to have heightened because of the present day family structure and relationships, parents working family has resulted in much less interaction with children. High rates of divorce, less time for parents to devote to their children, leaving children to child care facilities, using television for baby sitting are some other factors. Parenthood, in the urban context, generally is driven by ambition. In their eagerness to ensure that their children outperform others, they forget in the process that their children need to be good human beings as well.

The school personnel as well as parents should know that parents' involvement in education of their children positively influences their academic achievement, attitudes and values. Studies have shown that when parents are involved in the school, children learn better, get better grades, have more positive attitudes toward school and work and are likely to exhibit more positive behaviours. The implications for involving parents in value education in schools should therefore not be overlooked.

Enhancing parents' involvement in school is also in a way preparing the next generation of parents – those young students in middle and secondary schools to learn about the responsibilities of being a parent. There are certain barriers which come in the way of partnership between home and school. Poverty and illiteracy are the major blocks.

Many parents do not have the right kind of knowledge of what goes in schools. The discrepancy or the conflict between what is learnt in the school and what is learnt at home puts another barrier. Another major factor particularly in metropolitan cities is that many working parents do not have time to share work resulting in much less interaction with DEPFE, NCERT children as well as with school. Among poor communities, the problem is that children are expected to perform certain household chores that are crucial for the survival of the family.

Most parents believe that schools should make their children learn what is good, what is bad and that schools need to teach values and pro-social behaviours. This frame work calls for empowering parents, to involve parents and support parents in value oriented education of their wards. Here are some guidelines. The barriers to effective partnership should be thoroughly explored which may vary with socio-economic level, work schedule of parents, time and transportation. Special attention to this effect in all communication about the school's efforts on value education programmes should be given to parents.

Schools personnel need to communicate effectively and regularly with parents regarding school efforts in helping children learn and acquire good habits and values. Communication relates to three different types of issues:

(i) Feedback of student's performance and ability.

(ii) Feedback of student's needs and behaviour.

(iii) Communication of school policies.

While the first one always takes priority. The third one is hardly communicated to parents. In the present day world of fast communication, schools have many ways to communicate with the parents. School personnel need to have greater knowledge and awareness of students' family structure, particularly, if students come from dysfunctional family arrangement. They need to communicate frequently and effectively.

Schools must have written policy regarding family involvement in school governance and activities, need to review the Parent Teacher interaction (PTA) to make these work constructively, to discuss issues not just about the learning, but also about the parenting styles, communication styles with students and the need for modeling good values. What is important with these meetings is that there should not only happen when there are problems and these should not become the forums for complaints on both sides but these should be for appreciation or remediation? Then these forums could be used for discussion of school performance, its philosophy and for helping parents to become aware of efforts towards the value education. The quality of interaction is very important. It should go beyond passive listening to each other.

Parents and teachers can both work together to deal with certain issues such as negative peer pressures, violence exposure to media, excessive parental worry about the competition in the external world, syllabus load on children, dealing with stress among students, clarity about their own value system vis-à-vis efforts of schools and the kind of values they would like them to foster. Home school partnership framework must also include media literacy programme for parents and students which can help parents how best to monitor the programme that children can watch. To inform about the harmful effects of watching too much violence, crime which has detrimental effect of children and youths. Such programmes can help parents understand the positive aspects of television as well as adverse effects of television programming and how these can lead to degradation and erosion of values.

Schools can create an inventory of parent's skills and experiences and find out the kinds of volunteer work that parents can do in schools and how they can be involved in promoting the values. If school want, an inventory about the parents as resource and part of the community can be prepared. Parents can also take the role of volunteers to help the school in helping out with routine daily task in administration or in academics. These can only happen only with their continuous interaction. These interactions will ultimately help parents to become more involved and develop their ownership in the school.

Teachers' role is very vital in molding the future of a country and, as such, it is considered the noblest profession. Teachers are the ideals to their pupils. An educational institute should not be just confined to teaching and learning but it should be considered as a place where consciousness is aroused and illumined; soul is purified and strengthened. It is the place where the seeds of discipline, devotion and commitment are planted and fostered with deliberate efforts. A constructive companionship between teachers and students has to be developed. Gurus like: Parshuram, Bhishma and Drona influenced their students by practicing what they preached (Thakur, 2007). In a nutshell, a teacher in real sense is one who himself practices the human values. He should walk his talk to leave an ever lasting impression in the minds of students.

Unfortunately, today the 'personality' of the teachers has deteriorated. The society now, accords a low status to teachers; this profession has been highly depleted and demoralized owing to certain evils that have crept in this noble profession such as: castism, modernization, political influence, corruption and other unfair practices. Once upon a time, this institution which was esteemed highly and was considered as temple of learning (Gurukul) has now become one more, easy source of earning money. Incertain cases, the personality of the teachers has turned too dubious. They lack moral fiber and spiritual elegance and their behaviour has become highly suspicious, corrupt, degrading and disgusting. Some teachers relentlessly opt for this profession just for the sake of monetary benefits and to gain power and position, rather than for the integrity and sanctity of the profession. There was a time when a teacher was considered next to God.

In the modern era, we see a large number of teachers often making money by unfair or foul means. They are unscrupulous and resort to unfair means for making fast dough through indifference in teaching and conducting private tuition classes for extra income. This has led to malpractices in examinations by students and, in some cases, by teachers also. Besides this, we find considerable number of teachers addicted to smoking, drinking liquor and gambling. Therefore, how can such teachers impart values to the students? It is a recognised fact that teachers with awful habits working in education institutions cannot reflect positive teaching values in the classroom.

The success of any educational system depends on the quality of the teachers which, in turn, depends on the effective reaching-learning process in a class room. Teachers' performance is the most crucial input in the field of education. Therefore, teachers should be aware of the fact that their role is of vital significance for societal development and change. They must make an effort to light a candle instead of cursing the darkness and sow the seeds of value education with a great hope that they would disseminate their fragrance towards the creation of a just and new society as they spurt and blossom. Education without vision is waste, education without value is crime, and education without mission is life burden. A nation with atomic power is not a strong nation but a nation with people with strong character is indeed a strong nation. Therefore, for the sustainable human development as well as for the social growth, there is a need of value based education, spiritual education, ethical education, as well as need based education. Besides sustainable educational system, the special focus should be on inclusive growth with inclusive educational policies and programmes.

Ongoing Researches in the Field of Value Education – Present Scenario and Suggestions

Education is the vehicle of knowledge, self-preservation and success. Education not only gives us a platform to succeed, but also the knowledge of social conduct, strength, character and self respect. The greatest gift education gives us is the knowledge of unconditional love and a set of values. These values include the simple difference between right and wrong, a belief in God, the importance of hard work and self respect. Education is a continuous learning experience, learning from people, learning from success and failures, learning from leaders and followers and then growing up to be the person we are meant to be.

Value based education is a threefold development of any individual of any gender and age, but most importantly of a child. Education tries to develop three aspects: physique, mentality and character. Even though physique and mentality are important, they are menaces without the third because character is the greatest of these. Education plays a huge role in precisely this area.

Value based education is a tool which not only provides us a profession which we can pursue but also a purpose in life. The purpose of our life is undoubtedly to know oneself and be ourselves. We cannot do it unless we learn to identify ourselves with all that lives. It is very aptly said that: 'Know thyself' was written over the portals of the antique world. Over the portal of the new world, 'Be thyself' shall be written". Education gives us this very knowledge, the most supreme knowledge of knowing oneself, which helps us to make our life better and purposeful.

The objective of education in a country like India, which has a glorious heritage and can boast of diversity in geography, culture, values and beliefs very rarely seen in this wide world, should be to educate a student of the value system which is indispensable to live a successful life. There has been a lapse in our value system which the educational institutes should inculcate in a student – that is why there are increased incidences of teenage pregnancies, MMS scandals, student prostitution and academic pressure related suicides.

Today, the education imparted to the schools and colleges is almost limited to the finding of ways and means of earning of 'Bread and Butter'. It is indeed obvious that people in general wish education to be base on what they could garner monetary benefit. It won't be wrong to say that monetary considerations are the one which dictates the choosers of education today. Students are made to believe that by developing the ability to gather, store and retrieve vast information, they become educated. Education is not the amount of information that is stored into one's brain and remained hazy throughout life. Swami Vevekanand, one of the renowned socio-religious reformers of 19th century India rightly pointed out "Education is not the amount of information that is put into your brain and runs riot there, undigested all your life. We must have life building, man-making and character making assimilation of ideas".

Education without moral value will only fashion lop-sided personalities who may become rich in material possession but will remain poor in self-understanding, peace and social concern. It is indeed true that excess of knowledge and power, without moral makes man devils. In recent past we have seen man in uniform caught red-handed for involving in drug smuggling, raping of vegetable seller by those who are supposed to protect her, doctor killing his own daughter, sex scandal involving high profiled priest of Ashram etc. All these are the sign of moral degeneration.

The main causes of moral degeneration seems to be the lack of respect for the sanctity of human life, breakdown of parental control of children in families, breaking of the law and total disregard for rules and regulations. Crime and corruption, abuse of alcohol and drugs, abuse of women and children and other vulnerable members of society and lack of respect for other people and property are also very cause of moral degeneration. Why very often do the boarders in residential schools fight amongst themselves? Why students are not showing respect to the teachers? Let us take this an example. There is something wrong on the parts of the officials because such incidents are taking place quite very often. That means officials are not delivering their duty instead they are involving some other activities for their own interest and enjoyment. Perhaps this has come to the knowledge of the students who identifies the weakness of the authority and their officials. Those so called Principals and teachers, wearing the veil of honest Principals/Head masters and teachers are actually spoiling the teaching community. There are incidents students boozing at night in the residential schools at the very nose of the Principal but the respected Principal remains silent because he himself is so corrupt morally and always remains busy thinking how to earn easy money.

One of the best remedies to all these problems is value education. One must not forget that education provides us the platform to success. It is a continuous learning experience, learning from people, learning from success and failures, learning from leaders and followers and then growing up to be the person we are meant to be. Education is a process of grooming the learner to good life. But in the present day system of education there seems to be a 'moral vacuum'. Truly speaking, education devoid of moral character leads to criminality and educated persons have wider opportunity to indulge in crimes and that too committing them most efficiently and sophisticatedly. The value of truth, selflessness, impartiality, justice and service to mankind are drifting away from our life. People started believing in muscles and money power as a means to final solution to all problems.

Today one sees everywhere grossness and general insensitivity to finer feelings with the sole object of life being to make oneself as comfortable materially as one can. Today there is no respect for humanity-killing, murdering, raping, looting, drug trafficking, kidnapping for ransom etc., become common phenomena. In other word, crime, violence, cruelty, greed and apathy to human suffering have permeated to all aspects of our life-political, economic and social pursuit of material wealth and selfish end at any cost has become ultimate goal of life. There is great crisis in our society. Narrow mindedness, communalist, linguistic and regionalist outlooks have divided the people and come in the way of developing a unified national outlook. All the problems cannot be tackled through piece meal efforts. What we need under the current situation is a drastic change in our very outlook on life, which could be brought about by value education imparted systematically right from the primary level. In today's schools and colleges we see a large number of teachers who are more after making money by fair or foul means. Such unscrupulous teachers make fast money through indifference in classroom teaching and conducting mass private tuition classes. This has led to all sorts of malpractices in examinations. Teachers are less bothered about imparting the true spirit of education instead taking more interest in how to mint money. How can one expect good products from such educational establishment? How such teachers can be entrusted with teaching great values to the students who are considered to be the backbone of future nation.

We are in vicious circle-unless we inculcate values in school life and college life we cannot get value-oriented teachers in future. On the other hand so long as school administrators and teachers with bad habits are working in schools and colleges, value education cannot be effectively carried out. The moral values present a true perspective of the development of any society or nation. They tell us to what extent a society or nation has developed itself. Values are virtues, ideals and qualities on which actions and beliefs are based. Values are guiding principles that shape our world outlook, attitudes and conduct. Values however are either innate or acquired. Innate values are our inborn divine virtues such as love, peace, happiness, mercy and compassion as well as the positive moral qualities such as respect, humanity, tolerance, responsibility, co-operation, honesty and simplicity.

To solve all these type problems it is necessary to know the main causes of the above problems. We know today children are tomorrow's citizens. If we give good education to the present day children, the future of the next generations will be well. In my view education is the means through which all types of problems can be solved to a great extent. As we are passing through the 21st century, the use of the application of science and technology in proper way to solve all issues of non-moral and value things is essential. The main objective of the study is to inculcate moral and value based education in schools and colleges and to know the attitude of students towards moral values.

Students should be taught to cater life goals and good personal character. Students should be taught that our world is at peace if not involved the human interference. It is mankind who can make this world of ours free from war and conflict. People should be taught to understand meaning and value of life, happiness, equality, self-respect, family security, harmony, national security etc. Yes, indeed the role of the parents should also not to be forgotten. Every parent must teach their children value of life, mannerism, etiquette, self-respect and empathy.

The present social scenario is so pathetic and barbaric that we came across barbaric incidents every now and day. Due to the absence of moral education youths of today are unable to control their mind and begin to unleash a web disorder and lawlessness in the society which hard hit those sections of the society who are poor and innocent.

Hogan (1973) believes that moral behaviour is determined by five factors:

1. *Socialization*: Becoming aware as a child of society's and parents' rules of conduct for being good.
2. *Moral Judgment*: Learning to think reasonably about our own ethics and deliberately deciding on our own moral standards.
3. *Moral Feelings:* The internalization of our moral beliefs to the degree that we feel shame and guilt when we fail to do what we 'should'.
4. *Empathy*: The awareness of other people's situation, feelings, and needs so that one is compelled to help those in need.
5. *Confidence and Knowledge*: Knowing the steps involved in helping others and believing that one is responsible for and capable of helping.

M. K., Gandhi remarked that: 'if wealth is lost nothing is lost', 'if health is lost something is lost', 'if character is lost everything is lost', 'best of all things is character'.

Today we are facing so many problems such as: population problem, poverty, terrorism, proxy war, corruption crime against women, climate change and so on and so forth. Therefore, teaching of value education by untainted and uncorrupted teachers with high moral ethics is the call of the hour. Education is a weapon, whose effect depends on who holds it and at whom it is aimed. Why do we need value education? For instance if a highly qualified, well-employed person does not know how to behave properly, all that he or she does has little meaning and will not serve him or her well. Fruitful education is the kind used for our welfare as well as that of others. This can only happen when you have both academic and value education.

Values are usually influenced by the changing philosophical ideologies, cultural and religious perspectives, social, political and geographical conditions. In modern emerging society, there has been a revolutionary change in the field of values due to many factors in addition to the influence of modern culture, industrialization, modernization, urbanisation, globalisation and multinationals.

Values are the guiding principles, decisive in day to day behaviours as also is critical life situations. Values are a set bring of principles or standards of behaviour. Values are regarded desirable, important and held in high esteem by a particular society in which a person lives.. Value education refers to a programme of planned educational action aimed at the development of value and character. Every action and thought of ours leaves an impression in our mind. These impressions determine in our behaviour at a given moment and our responses to a given situation. The sum total of all our impressions is what determines our character. The past has determined the present and even so the present our present thoughts and actions will shape our future. This is a key principle governing personality development. The human values are resolved having lasting impact necessary for bringing about change in thought and conduct, in the 21st century.

"If there is righteousness in the heart there will be beauty in character If there is beauty in character There will be harmony in the home When there is harmony in the home There will be order in the nation When there is order in the nation There will be peace in the world". Value education means inculcating in the children a sense humanism, a deep concern for the well being of others and the nation. This can be accomplished only when we instill in the children a deep feeling of commitment to values that would build this country and bring back to the people pride in work that brings order, security and assured progress.

5 Essentiality of Value and Peace

Values and Peace – The Need of the Hour

Education is defined as acquiring skills. There are many different ways to be educated and many subjects that can be studied. School is not the only place or setting in which we can learn or get an education. For some families, it means graduating from high school; others believe an education means receiving a bachelor's degree or certification from a good trade school. While there are many ways to define education, most people agree that the more education a person achieves, the higher their wages, generally speaking. Has this changed in the last 10 years? If so, how much of a contrast in pay is there? What other aspects of employment are impacted by receiving an education? This article will attempt to answer these questions as well as provide further evidence of the importance of an education in today's economy. An education has always been important and now it is more valuable than ever.

The following set of ten values should be borne in mind and to be inculcated in the minds of the learners as well as those who teach them.

1. Tolerance and understanding (Accepting other people's differences and being aware of others).
2. Respect (Treating others with consideration and regard).
3. Responsibility – personal, social, civic and environmental (Being accountable for and in charge of a course of action – responsibility for one's own actions, including the exercise of self-discipline; responsibility for the way in which one interacts and co-operates with others especially for resolving differences in constructive, non-violent and peaceful ways; responsibility for one's role in and contribution to society; and responsibility for one's own role in the maintenance and preservation of the environment).
4. Social justice (Being committed to the pursuit and protection of the common good where all persons are entitled to legal, social and economic fair treatment).
5. Excellence (Seeking to accomplish something noteworthy and admirable individually and collectively, and performing at one's best).
6. Care (Caring for self and showing interest in, concern for and caring for others).
7. Inclusion and trust (Being included and including others, listening to one another's thoughts and feelings actively and creating a climate of mutual confidence).
8. Honesty (Being truthful and sincere, committed to finding and expressing the truth, requiring truth from others, and ensuring consistency between words and deeds).
9. Freedom (Enjoying all the rights and privileges of citizenship free from unnecessary interference or control, and standing up for the rights of others; ensuring a balance between rights and responsibilities).
10. Being ethical (Acting in accordance with generally agreed rules and/or standards for right [moral] conduct or practice).

Basic education aims to produce children who are happy with themselves and with others; to create an approach to knowledge that children can use and develop throughout their lives as they learn to know, to do, to be and to live together with others (UNESCO 2002, Delors 1996). In the basic education phase is where life long lasting attitudes towards learning are developed, this education phase is indispensable as it enables students to choose what they want and participate in the construction of the collective future. On the other hand, the school as educative institution is facing a stage of decay due to the disparity between what it should provide, according to its capacities and aims, and what it is actually providing (YurÈn 1995). Values education is presented as an alternative to the deterioration process in the school and core in the basic education phase.

Human value is an academic behaviour through which progress of individual, society, nation and international understanding are created. Education aims at all round development of human beings, therefore Cognitive, Cognative and Affective domains are taken to task at learning levels for individual progress. By exchange of subject information, development in cognitive domain is easily possible. Application of skills is cognative domain and is related to fixing of human values and its preservation. Until an emotional feeling does not exit, an individual cannot achieve wisdom. This important part is neglected through curriculum. Thus inculcation of value education is for emotional development.

Education is a continuous process of refinement, research and realisation, and must equip our youth to deal with the pressing problems of today and those which arise in future. As H.G. Wells put it: “Human history becomes more and more a race between education and catastrophe”. Unless we strengthen the education in its content and relevance and instill a sincere concern for human welfare, catastrophe cannot be avoided.

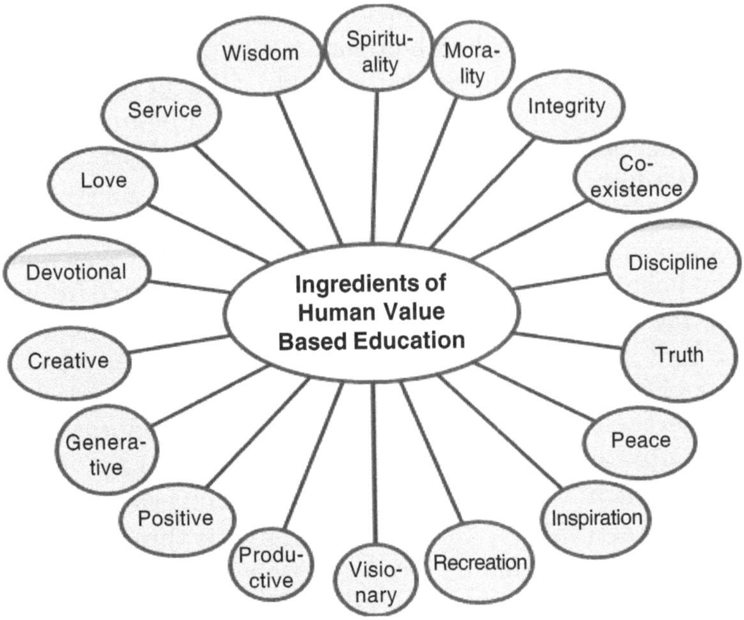

Almost every one of the men and women now governing and managing national and international governments and institutions was once a student in a school, a college or a university. Their performance today is clearly a reflection of the way they were educated. Had their education given them all that is required, their performance would be as we require. "To educate a man in mind and not in morals is to educate a menace to society", said U.S. President Theodore Roosevelt. And in the same vein, our own Nehruji declared: "If all is well with colleges and universities, all is well with the nation".

Only a value-based education can give our youth the altruistic and benevolent sense of living for others; as Swami Vivekananda said, 'They alone live who live for others'. We should always bear in mind that by helping others we help ourselves. By bringing prosperity to others we ourselves prosper. Conversely, we cannot give pain to another without giving pain to ourselves, and a loss caused to another is necessarily a loss to oneself.

There is a solution to the problems of the youth. The solution lies in re-establishing the self-confidence of the youth, in showing them the way of regaining their faith in themselves. With this, not only the individual but also the society rises to the heights of great achievement. When an individual becomes aware of his own tremendous potentialities, when he realises that he himself is the architect of his future, he tries honestly to come up in life just like a man who falls to the ground will use the ground itself for support to stand up.

Good values are the spontaneous manifestations of a sound character and values form the central pole around which our actions, desires and ambitions are organized. Values guide our behaviour and give meaning to our existence. Values assist us to take right decisions and make choices. Values give direction and firmness to life and help us to be morally sound. Values set goals for achievements and they motivate, define and colour all our activities in cognitive, affective and cognative domains.

Bibliography

Robert Ehrlich Perspectives on Nuclear War and Peace Education. Greenwood Press, 1987.

Linda Rennie Forcey; Ian Murray Harris Peace Building for Adolescents: Strategies for Educators and Community Leaders Peter Lang, 1999.

Haim A. Gordon Dance, Dialogue, and Despair: Existentialist Philosophy and Education for Peace in Israel. University of Alabama, 1986.

Volker Franke. Preparing for Peace: Military Identity, Value Orientations, and Professional Military Education Praeger Publishers, 1999.

Harriet Hyman Alonso. Peace as a Women's Issue: A History of the U.S. Movement for World Peace and Women's Rights Syracuse University Press, 1993.

John Somerville. The Peace Revolution: Ethos and Social Process. Greenwood Press, 1975. Between War and Peace: A Handbook for Peace Workers.

Conflict Resolution Education: A Solution for Peace

Lincoln, Melinda G. Communications and the Law, Vol. 23, No. 1, March 2001.

Deutsch, M. (1949). A Theory of Co-operation and Competition. Human Relations, 2, 129-152.

Johnson, D. W. (1970). Social Psychology of Education. New York: Holt, Rinehart and Winston.

Johnson, D. W. (2003). Social Interdependence: The Interrelationships among Theory, Research, and Practice. American Psychologist, 58(11).

Johnson D. W., and Johnson, F. (2009). Joining Together: Group Theory and Group Skills (9th Ed.). Boston: Allyn and Bacon.

Johnson, D. W., and Johnson, R. (1974). Instructional Goal Structure: Co-operative, Competition, or Individualistic. *Review of Educational Research*, 44, 213-240.

Johnson, D. W., and Johnson, R. (1979). Conflict in the Classroom: Controversy and Learning. *Review of Educational Research*, 49.

Johnson, D. W., and Johnson, R. (1989). Co-operation and Competition: Theory and Research. Edina, MN: Interaction Book Company.

Johnson, D. W., and Johnson, R. (1994). Co-operative Learning and American Values. The Co-operative Link, 9(3).

Johnson, D. W., and Johnson, R. (1996). Conflict Resolution and Peer Mediation Programmes in Elementary and Secondary Schools: A Review of the Research. *Review of Educational Research*, 66(4).

Johnson, D. W., and Johnson, R. (1996). Co-operative Learning and Traditional American Values. NASSP Bulletin, 80(579).

Johnson, D. W., and Johnson, R. (2000). Civil Political Discourse in a Democracy: The Contribution of Psychology.

Peace and Conflict: *Journal of Peace Psychology*, 6(4).

Johnson, D. W., and Johnson, R. (2000). Co-operative Learning, Values, and Culturally Plural Classrooms.

In M. Leicester, C. Modgill, and S. Modgil (Eds.), Values, the Classroom, and Cultural Diversity, London.

Cassell. Johnson, D. W., and Johnson, R. (2000, June). Teaching Students to be Peace-makers: Results of Twelve Years of Research. Paper presented at the Society for the Psychological Study of Social Issues Convention, Minneapolis, MN.

Johnson, D. W., and Johnson, R. (2003). Controversy and Peace Education. *Journal of Research in Education*, 13(1), 71-91.

Johnson, D. W., and Johnson, R. (2003b). Field Testing Integrative Negotiations. Peace and Conflict: *Journal of Peace Psychology*, 9(1), 39-68.

Johnson, D. W., and Johnson, R. (Eds.). (2003). Frontiers in Research: Peace Education [Special Section]. *Journal of Research in Education*, 13(1), 39-91.

Johnson, D. W., and Johnson, R. (2005). Democratic Decision-Making, Political Discourse, and Constructive Controversy. *The Co-operative Link*, 20(1), 3.

Johnson, D. W., and Johnson, R. (2005). New Developments in Social Interdependence Theory. Genetic, Social, and General Psychology Monographs, 131(4), 285-358.

Johnson, D. W., and Johnson, R. (Guest Eds.). (2005). Peace Education. Theory into Practice, 44(4).

Johnson, D. W., and Johnson, R. (2005). Teaching Students to be Peace-makers (4th Ed.). Edina, MN: Interaction Book Company.

Johnson, D. W., and Johnson, R. T. (2006). Peace Education for Consensual Peace: The Essential Role of Conflict Resolution. *Journal of Peace Education*, 3(2), 147-174.

Johnson, D. W., and Johnson, R. T. (2007). Creative Controversy: Intellectual Challenge in the Classroom (4th Ed.). Edina, MN: Interaction Book Company.

Johnson, D. W., Johnson, R., and Holubec, E. (2002). Circles of learning (5th Ed.). Edina, MN: Interaction Book Company.

Johnson, D. W., Johnson, R., and Holubec, E. (2008). Co-operation in the Classroom (7th Ed.). Edina, MN: Interaction Book Company.

Johnson, D. W., Johnson, R., and Smith, K. (2000). Constructive Controversy: The Educative Power of Intellectual Conflict. Change, 32(1), 28-37.

Johnson, D. W., and Lewicki, R. (1969). The Initiation of Super Ordinate Goals. *Journal of Applied Behavioural Science*, 5, 9-24.

Merton, R. K. (1957). Social Theory and Social Structure. New York: Free Press.

Poon, M., Pike, R., and Tjosvold, D. (2001). Budget Participation, Goal Interdependence and Controversy: A Student of a Chinese Public Utility. *Management Accounting Research*, 12, 101-118.

Sherif, M. (1966). In Common Predicament. Boston: Houghton-Mifflin.

Snell, R. S., Tjosvold, D., and Su, F. S. (in press). Resolving Ethical Conflicts at Work through Co-operative Goals and Constructive Controversy in the People's Republic of China. *Asia Pacific Journal of Management.*

Tjosvold, D. (1982). Effects of the Approach to Controversy on Superiors' Incorporation of Subordinates' Information in Decision-Making. *Journal of Applied Psychology*, 67, 189-193.

Tjosvold, D., and Sun, H. F. (2002). Understanding Conflict Avoidance: Relationship, Motivations, Actions, and Consequences. *International Journal of Conflict Management*, 13(2), 142-164.

Index